Waylon Taylor

If We Dared!

IF
WE
DARED!

Chester E. Swor

BROADMAN PRESS Nashville, Tennessee

© 1961 · BROADMAN PRESS
Nashville, Tennessee
All rights reserved
International copyright secured

Ninth Printing

ISBN: 0-8054-5110-2
4251-10

Library of Congress catalog card number 61-12417
Printed in the United States of America
2.Je7119

DEDICATION

To the valiant ones who have helped
and who are helping Christians everywhere to grow up "unto the measure
of the stature of the fulness of
Christ"—ministers, teachers, parents,
counselors, and other friends, whose
examples and whose efforts have beck-
oned us to "come up higher" on the
mountain trail of Christian maturity

Beyond the Star

I looked long at a star,
Deeply, and long,
Till suddenly I looked beyond the star
For one transcendent instant, and caught a glimpse
Of God.

And now I go with astonishment in my heart
And sorrow,
Knowing that the earth is too narrow,
And the sky too low,
And the souls of men too small
To contain so much vastness
Of love.

God,
Help us grow.[1]

JANE MERCHANT

Preface

BECAUSE OF THE GRACIOUS AND GENerous acceptance of my initial volume, *Very Truly Yours,* I am emboldened now to offer another group of devotional messages in this second volume.

These messages, too, have come from the crucible of everyday living—my own, and that of so many other people whose experiences are known to me. Therefore, they are not messages concerning untried or unapplied principles; rather, they are messages built around the principles originally taught and practiced by Jesus, demonstrated by his followers through the centuries, and translated into the experiences of so many people of our own day.

The great hope of IF WE DARED! is expressed in the supplication, "God, help us grow," the concluding words of the beautiful title poem facing the Preface. The messages of this book have been written in the fervent hope that they will challenge Christians to *dare* to follow the example and to translate the teachings of Jesus into the fabric of character and conduct; for, in so doing, they shall be in a continuing state of growth toward spiritual maturity.

It is the author's conviction that the status of Christianity in our world today would be so much more vast in scope and significance if Christians of our own and earlier days had dared to follow Jesus in every facet of life. He believes, too, that if Christians will dare to follow Jesus in all of life's relationships, an amazing transformation will occur in individual lives and, eventually, in our entire society.

The author's consuming hope, therefore, is that many readers of these chapters will dare to shake off whatever lethargy, fears, or self-satisfaction may have kept them in the past from daring to commit themselves without reservation to the example and teachings of Jesus; and that, regardless of the cost or consequences, Paul's "For to me to live is Christ" will become the ideal and the determinant in the lives of many Christians who read these messages. Every Christian who dares to make such a committal will find that life will never be the same again!

In the preparation of this volume, as in my earlier one, I have been aided by a great concourse of people who have contributed to my life the rich treasures of their own lives. Some of these cherished people have shared insights and experiences which appear in these pages; others have urged me to write again and have prayed diligently for my efforts; still others along the way have given assurance, confidence, and the superlative gift of friendship. My gratitude to all who have made this book possible is very great.

CHESTER E. SWOR

Contents

PART ONE

Two Hopes

Two Hills

Two Gardens

Two Prayers

In Which
The Christian Is Invited to Ex-
amine Himself in the Light of
the Example and Teachings of
Jesus Concerning Surrender, For-
giveness, Obedience, and Prayer

1. Two Hopes

Behold, I stand at the door, and knock: if any man hear my voice, and open the door, I will come in to him.
REVELATION 3:20
Ye are the light of the world. . . . Let your light so shine before men, that they may see your good works, and glorify your Father which is in heaven.
MATTHEW 5:14,16

THOUGH THERE ARE MANY HOPES which Jesus has for our lives, it is not an oversimplification to say that these hopes may be combined into two great ones: he hopes to do some things *to* us, and he hopes to do some things *through* us. From the very nature of the things which he wishes to do through us, it is evident that he cannot do them until he has been permitted to do to us what he wishes to do.

I

Simply put, the things which Jesus wishes to do *to* us are these: he wishes to come into our lives to perform *regeneration*—to give us the new birth, to make us new creatures in him; thereafter, he wishes to be permitted to possess our lives to a degree which will make possible *transformation*—to be permitted to remold, to remake our lives so completely that everywhere and all the time people will take knowledge that we have been with Jesus.

The coming of Jesus into our hearts and the performance of regeneration are inseparable. He does not come in as a visitor or on probation. If he comes into our hearts at all, he comes as Saviour, the giver of eternal life. And, as many readers of these pages know, he comes into the human heart only when asked by the individual who, with repentance toward sin and with faith in Jesus, *wants* him to come in. This is the experience variously referred to as *regeneration, salvation, the new birth, being born again.* Without this experience the individual, though he be baptized and enrolled in church membership, is not a Christian. So, the first thing which Jesus wants to do *to* us is to come into our hearts to bring new life, eternal life, which is the power of God unto salvation.

Beyond this initial experience, however, many Christians move slowly in surrendering the control of their lives to Christ, and so many become definitely obstinate in this regard. Jesus cannot remold and remake us after his will unless we permit him to control every area of our lives. The failure of such a large number of Christians in our nation to yield this control to Jesus has brought a tragic result: so many non-Christians cannot see or feel any differences in the lives of great throngs of Christians and do not, therefore, feel any need to become followers of Jesus.

Observers cannot see the experience of regeneration, for it is purely an inner experience of the heart. They can see transformation, however, and they are always impressed deeply to see such changes in character and conduct that Christians seem to be "different persons." The oft-repeated reminder, "What you are speaks so much louder than what you say, I can't hear a word of it," can be revised happily to say, "What you are speaks so much more wonderfully than what you say, I hear every word of it!"

II

The Christian who does not permit Christ to perform transformation of his life misses his only opportunity to taste Christianity at its most gratifying state, and he misses the opportunity to have his own life turned into a masterpiece.

The really happy Christians of any age are those who have permitted Christ to mold and make their lives after his wish until, in keeping with the sentiments of a well-known hymn, Christ holds o'er their beings absolute sway. The exquisite joy of close fellowship with Jesus, the thrill of seeing and feeling God's power flow through a surrendered life, the amazing accomplishments of miraculous nature with which the surrendered Christian becomes familiar—these are some of the thrills which come to the life of anyone who has permitted Christ to fulfil his hope of transforming the

Christian's life. The nonsurrendered Christian is likely to be the miserable one: close enough to know the claims of the lordship of Christ, unwilling to pay the price; yearning for maximum joy, unwilling to admit that it comes from maximum surrender.

Peter was so amazed by the transforming touch of Christ in his life, that he cried out upon Christ's asking whether or not other disciples wished to turn aside from following him, "Lord, to whom shall we go? thou hast the words of eternal life" (John 6:68). A twentieth-century Christian who had yielded his life to the lordship of Christ after years of stubborn resistance and detours of heartbreaking nature said: "I am amazed that I fought so long against my own best welfare! Though I tasted of all the cups the world offered, I have found nothing to compare with my present relationship to Christ in pure joy, deep peace, and real thrills!"

The canvas' only hope of becoming a masterpiece is that it surrender its surface completely to the plan of the artist; but when it does so, it becomes a masterpiece. The only hope of marble and wood to become masterpieces of statuary and wood carving is to surrender themselves entirely to the plan and procedure of the sculptor and the carver. Even the diamond's hope of becoming a sparkling masterpiece rests in its being completely surrendered to the cutting and designing of the diamond cutter. Expensive musical instruments do not show their real worth until they are at the disposal of master artists who know how to turn their potentialities into great music. Without a full surrender on the part of an object or a person, there would be no masterpieces of art or life.

A brilliant young lawyer who had been a Christian for many years, but who had not permitted Christ to accomplish the hope of transformation in his life, met another young professional man who had permitted that fulfilment of Christ's hope in his life. The lawyer's keen mind discerned the difference and the reason for the difference. He, too, paid the price of full surrender, and the result of the transforming touch of Jesus in his life was so great that he became one of the most inspiring Christians in a large metropolitan area. His life became a masterpiece—a challenge to those who needed to move toward surrender, and a reproof to Christians who continue to frustrate Christ's hope to do that second wonderful thing to their lives.

III

Jesus made so clear his hope of getting *through* our lives to touch and change people and circumstances around us. In one instance he reminded his followers that they were the "salt of the earth," but added the reminder that the salt is useless if it loses its "savor." Salt changes the flavor of the dish into which it is put. It adds a zest and a palatability which increase the attractiveness of food. Think of the many dishes of food which you would not even like if the salt were omitted. Salt is expected to change the flavor of its surroundings.

One Christian in a shop or store or office or club or

barracks or family or any other group can change the spiritual flavor of the entire group. One secretary in a stenographers' pool of fifty young women lived her Christianity so winsomely that the supervisor noticed a marked change in the atmosphere of the entire group before the first month of that secretary's work was finished. One young man, living for four years in a university fraternity, changed the atmosphere of that group so completely that the transformation seemed almost a miracle to the campus. One boy in a non-Christian family permitted Christ to touch and transform his life, and all the members of that family came to faith in Jesus. A high school student body of 1800 students experienced a remarkable transformation in spirit, led primarily by the glorious example of a dedicated Christian student.

Jesus reminded his followers, also, "Ye are the light of the world." Light dispels darkness and illumines what otherwise would be dark and forbidding. Even one tiny candle in an otherwise darkened room makes a major difference. Regardless of the age or ability of the Christian, he can make a luminous difference in his surroundings.

A boot trainee had the courage to read his Bible and to pray in his barracks nightly, and the courage to live his Christianity consistently and winsomely every day. Before the end of boot training, his entire group of barracks buddies joined him in nighttime devotions on their own initiative. One high school boy, working with a street crew in the summer months, lived his

Christianity so luminously in the grimy, hot chores of the summer that a transformation occurred in the thinking, talking, and attitudes of his fourteen associates on the crew.

Given an opportunity to get through an individual or group of Christians, Christ can touch and transform the most difficult situation. But we must remind ourselves over and over again that he cannot get *through* us until he has been permitted to do *to* us what he wants to do. Missionaries have found it very difficult so often to get the real spirit of Christ through to non-Christian groups, because these groups have been so hurt by the inconsistent practices of Christians who were in their countries in connection with business and industry, or because they have appraised American Christianity on the basis of our movies and on the basis of the behavior of our people who travel as tourists in their countries. Christ cannot get through people who are not Christlike.

IV

But, since the greatest hope and joy of Christ's heart occur in the salvation of the individual, it follows that the greatest accomplishment of his reaching through us is realized in our bringing unsaved people to him. Someone pointed out long ago that when a transformed person goes to speak to an unsaved person, his argument is 95 per cent won by his life before he ever opens his mouth to speak. It is imperative that we permit Jesus, who redeemed us, to transform us, so that he may reach through us to bring redemption and transformation to others.

Very early in the history of Christianity the thrilling instances of Christ's reaching through transformed people began to occur. Andrew was used as the means through which Jesus reached to touch and save Peter. The Samaritan woman, saved in the memorable conversation with Jesus at the well, was used as the one through whom the message of the Messiah's coming was brought to a city. Philip was used as the means through which Jesus reached to touch the Ethiopian eunuch. Paul's salvation experience was facilitated by the triumphant life and death of Stephen. Through Paul a great concourse of people have felt the beckoning, regenerating, and transforming power of Christ.

On a university campus the "bad boy" of the student body was reached through the dedicated life of a fellow student. He, in turn, became a living proof of the saving and transforming power of Christ and won a great number of students to Christ. In one week he won seven! On another campus Christ reached through the life of a charming, dedicated girl to touch a devout Moslem with the realization that Christ's way is the better way. He became a Christian and returned to his homeland to face possible persecution, but to witness victoriously.

In one city an outstanding businessman was won, largely by the attractive Christian witness of his daughter. That same man now breathes a passion for lost people and is winning great numbers to faith in Jesus. Another businessman of almost incredible sin was won through the life and witness of an employee. His own life is now "Exhibit Number One" of the transforming power of Christ in that city.

Through the lives of dedicated wives Christ has so often reached to touch unsaved husbands; or unsaved wives have been reached through dedicated husbands. Through the consistent, attractive living of individuals or families, neighbors have been won to Christ. In short, when Christ has had the opportunity to do *to* us all that he wishes to do, his hope to reach others *through* us is easy of fulfilment.

So, there are those two hopes which Jesus has for your life and mine, and the second hope depends upon the fulfilment of the first hope. It is in order for every reader to ask, "In the light of the degree to which Jesus possesses and directs my life, am I fulfilling or frustrating those two hopes which he has for me?"

2. Two Hills

From Sermon on the Mount . . .

And seeing the multitudes, he went up into a mountain: and when he was set, his disciples came unto him: and he opened his mouth, and taught them, saying, ... Ye have heard that it hath been said, Thou shalt love thy neighbour, and hate thine enemy. But I say unto you, love your enemies, bless them that curse you, do good to them that hate you, and pray for them which despitefully use you, and persecute you.   MATTHEW 5:1–2,43–44

On Golgotha . . .

Then said Jesus, Father, forgive them; for they know not what they do.
LUKE 23:34

NOTICE TWO MEMORABLE HILLS: the hill on which Jesus sat to *teach* his amazing principle of Christian love and forgiveness, and the hill of Golgotha on which, while hanging in humiliation and pain, his spirit reached out to *practice* the love and forgiveness which he had taught. It was then, as it has been through the centuries, measurably harder to practice the magnificent ideals of Christianity than to proclaim them; yet, Christ climbed both hills with glorious victory!

You and I have climbed that first hill, the hill on which we have heard and have assented to Christ's teachings of love and forgiveness. A large number of us, however, are finding it difficult to climb that second hill; and so many of us are not even trying. A highly talented and sensitive man, who had been tragically wronged, practically shouted to a counselor, "I can't love *that* person, and I won't even try!"

Though it is much harder to climb that second hill, we have no alternative to climbing it if we wish to translate Christianity into a living reality in our own lives, and if we wish our lives to show forth the proof that the hardest teachings of Jesus *can* be practiced. Furthermore, we shall never know the tremendous joy of thrilling victory until we have practiced these most difficult teachings of Jesus.

We need to admit at the outset of this study, however, that mere human strength is not adequate to the translation of these hard-to-achieve ideals into our lives. Our resolutions must be supported by the power which God will give to us if we *want* that power earnestly enough. It takes both God and man to accomplish the Christian teachings concerning love and forgiveness: man's resolution and effort, God's limitless and available power. With that combination there are three magnificent victories which we can achieve in climbing that second hill.

I

First, we *can* come to love unlovable people. Christ's listeners, as he delivered the Sermon on the Mount, must have been aghast at his saying, "But I say unto you, love your enemies." Not only had religion never taught that obligation, but, on first hearing, it must have seemed contradictory to all the impulses of human nature to try to love somebody who, by his own actions, had demonstrated his enmity toward you—perhaps even his desire to do great hurt to you. "Love *that* person? Ridiculous!" must have been the silent observation of some hearts in that crowd. Unfortunately, many Christians more than nineteen hundred years later entertain the same reaction.

If we are to come to love unlovable people, there will have to be a change of heart on our part, and it is in this change of heart that God's power is necessary. The first change which needs to come to some hearts is the change which regeneration makes: the experience of being born again, of becoming new creatures in Christ Jesus. Paul once hated the Christians with a passion and stood by, consenting to the death of Stephen. When he experienced the regenerating power of Christ in his heart on the Damascus road, he came into new power, new attitudes, and new desires which made possible his loving the very people he had once hated so vehemently.

Though one be called a Christian, he simply does not have access to the power which will make possible his loving unlovable people unless he has had a genuine experience of regeneration in his heart. That experience gives the Christian access to God, who, in turn, gives the individual the desire and the power to love beyond mere human affection.

But even Christians will not come to love difficult people until they obtain from God, through fervent wish and prayer, the ability to see those people through God's eyes. When that ability comes, there will be a change of heart toward unlovable people. That is the explanation of Jesus' ability to love people who were reprehensibly sinful or who, through their very actions, had classified themselves as his bitter enemies. Toward the benighted woman caught in adultery, toward the oft-sinning woman at the well of Sychar, toward dishonest Zacchaeus, toward obdurate and unresponsive Jerusalem, toward the rich young ruler who heard but did not follow, toward those who sought to trap him, and even toward those who crucified him, Jesus displayed a Christian love which had overcome normal revulsions and resentments. How did he do it?

Jesus simply looked at these people through the eyes of God, not through selfish, self-centered sensitiveness. In taking that look he was able to see things in their lives which touched the wellspring of compassion. He saw deep hungers, frustrations, perversions, misguided loyalties, immature spiritual insight, misdirected passions and emotions, and a sense of disappointment within them which caused them to cry out at others. Seeing these things brought an understanding as to why they acted as they did. On the heels of that understanding there came a deep sorrow for their unhappy condition; and on the heels of this compassionate sorrow there came a warm desire to help those who were not his friends. The understanding, the sorrow, and the desire to help led to his initiative to help. This was Christian love in action.

The formula for you and me is the same. We *can* come to love unlovable people, but we shall have to follow the formula. We need to pray that God will "lift us out of ourselves" to the point at which we, too, can look through God's eyes into the inner recesses of the hearts of these people whom normal human attitudes cause us to dislike. We shall come to such an insight if we try earnestly, through a spirit-led restudy of the teachings of Christ; through fervent prayer that God will illumine our hearts with a portion of his insight to these difficult people; and, at times, through a psychological study of the external indications of internal maladjustment. Then we, too, shall understand why these people act as they do; the understanding will lead to a poignant sorrow for their plight; the sorrow will lead to a desire to help; that desire translated into action will be a "flesh and blood" translation of Matthew 5:43–44.

A victory in this important regard will bring to us a thrill of nearness to Jesus not experienced by many Christians of our day and will release power into and through our lives which will bless others. A new reward awaits the Christian who dares to try.

II

We *can* come to forgive the "unpardonable." The first step in the Christian's achieving the victory of forgiving people whose actions have been reprehensible is to admit that it can be done. If the Christian closes the door by saying, "It's utterly impossible," he is not only robbing himself of the experience of trying, but he is saying, in effect, that the teachings of Jesus in this regard are impossible to achieve and that the example of Jesus in this matter was not meant to be obeyed by his followers.

Regardless of the baseness or vileness of the wrong done to the Christian, he *can* forgive. The question, therefore, is, "Does he *want* to forgive?" The plain truth is that some Christians virtually enjoy "wallowing" in a feeling of being wronged and rather selfishly cling to the role of being sinned against. Still others give way to the "eye for an eye" doctrine and feel that they must strike back a harder blow than the one given them. When the hawk of vengeance comes into the heart, the dove of forgiveness departs. When the unforgiving spirit is worsened by vengeful retaliation, the Christian not only has not solved his problem, he has created another problem—the problem of needing forgiveness by his enemy.

If, however, the Christian is willing to crucify selfish self in favor of Christlikeness, he will admit that these three things which Christ taught about forgiveness can be practiced:

1. *The Christian can forgive without number limit.* When one of Christ's most discerning followers asked if one should forgive a brother seven times, Christ replied, "Seventy times seven." We need to cease putting a ceiling on the forgiveness which we shall practice and realize, instead, that Christianity obligates us to keep on forgiving as long as contrite people ask forgiveness.

2. *The Christian can provide forgiveness in his heart before the wrongdoer or enemy even asks for it.* Look again at the example of Christ on the cross. Had that ugly, milling, reviling crowd asked for forgiveness or even thought of asking for it? No! Our Master provided the forgiveness then and there in his own heart, however. Any of that degrading crowd who never asked for that forgiveness could never say that it was not provided. You can forgive that enemy in your heart right now. Though he will not receive the beautiful gift of forgiveness until he asks for it, you and God will know that it has been provided in your heart.

3. *The Christian can grow to the point of wanting to measure his spirit of forgiveness according to the generosity of God's forgiveness toward him.* "Forgive us our sins; for we also forgive every one that is indebted to us" (Luke 11:4) actually invites God to use the same measure or lack of generosity toward us which we have used toward others. Translated into action, this prayer means that the Christian will not only forgive as God does, but that he will also emulate God in remembering no more the forgiven sins against people.

III

As Christians we can come not only to love the un-lovable and to forgive the unpardonable; we can come, also, to the superlative in love and forgiveness: *we can take the love and forgiveness to the unlovable and the unpardonable!* After having asked his followers to love their enemies, Jesus immediately requested that they translate this love into initiatives through praying for those people and by doing good things for those who had done evil to them (Matt. 5:43–44). What a victory over self to come to love the unlovable and to forgive the unpardonable! What a victory over false pride to convey that love in such unmistakable terms!

In Matthew 5:23–24 Christ makes clear, also, that the Christian should take the initiative in going to that person with whom his relationships are not what they ought to be, even if the Christian feels that he is un-questionably the one sinned against: "Therefore if thou bring thy gift to the altar, and there rememberest that thy brother hath ought against thee; Leave there thy gift before the altar, and go thy way; first be rec-onciled to thy brother, and then come and offer thy gift."

Christ was asking his followers to do no more than he had done and would continue to do. Neither he nor God had wronged the world; yet, the world was surely at enmity toward God. God so loved this enemy that he sent his choicest possession in an attempt to recon-cile the enemy, and Christ loved so much that he came without complaint. With neither invitation nor appreciation he continued to take the initiative toward people whose lives were affronting God every day. There he stood, offering an unmerited love, extending an unsought forgiveness!

Since it was not beneath the dignity of God's only begotten Son to take the initiative with love and forgiveness toward a frightful enemy, it should not be beneath your dignity and mine to take the initiative in carrying love and forgiveness to our enemies, in keeping with his specific request. Although the overwhelming majority of Christians do not follow the teaching and example of Jesus in this important area, those who do follow find a fellowship with him which brings a transformation into their lives; and their lives, in turn, bring an incomparable inspiration to others.

Have you ever climbed that second hill, the hill on which you practiced what your ear and heart had heard in his teaching on that first hill? Do you need to climb that second hill now? Though that second hill is so much harder to climb, its victory is so much more wonderful to possess. Those who have scaled the earth's great mountain peaks have achieved only a minor victory in comparison to the victory of Christians who have become mountain climbers in love and forgiveness.

IV

Is anybody in our day climbing that second hill? Their names may not be numerous, and their feats do not appear often in the columns of newspapers; yet there are some heroic ones who are achieving this glorious victory.

There is the man whose little daughter was ravished and murdered by a sadist, but who appealed through press and radio that people not prejudge or condemn too harshly the teen-ager who had committed the crime until all the factors governing his life were known. Furthermore, he announced that he had forgiven the murderer in his heart! Impossible? Not so, for one of our own fellow countrymen achieved that forgiveness within the year in which these lines are being written.

A wonderful woman who had been the victim of a very unjust family financial settlement kept on loving her malefactors, though she herself was put to many years of privation as a result of the injustice. She translated her love and forgiveness into action with continuing instances of returning good for evil, with continuing prayer for these wrongdoers, and with fervent efforts to win them to Christ. Once, at her own expense, she made a three-thousand-mile round trip to try to win one of them to Christ. Was that in the easy long ago or in our busy, tension-filled day? That, too, occurred in the year in which these lines are being written.

There is the American ex-serviceman who was in Corregidor, in the Bataan Death March, and in the enemy's prisons and salt mines through the 1942–45 period. He was lashed, underfed, overworked, and in so many other ways abused and humiliated by his captors for over three years. Upon his eventual release from protracted hospitalization in American hospitals he said: "I never permitted myself to hate my persecutors; for I knew that if I did, I could not let the love of Christ flow through me. Many of the guards asked why I didn't hate them; and, when I told them of the teachings of Christ, some of them began to read the Bible furtively. Now I want to take an engineering degree and go back to the land of my captors to help rebuild the wreckage of war and to be a good Christian witness!"

If you and I do not climb that second hill, we can never say that we *could not* climb it; the truth will be that we *would not* climb it. Today would be a fine time to begin the journey up that second hill!

3. Two Gardens

And the Lord God planted a garden eastward in Eden; and there he put the man whom he had formed.
GENESIS 2:8
Then cometh Jesus with them unto a place called Gethsemane.
MATTHEW 26:36

W_RITERS OF BOTH POETRY AND PROSE have pointed out that two gardens have influenced the destinies of mankind more than all other gardens in history combined. They are the Garden of Eden and the garden of Gethsemane.

These writers have pointed out that in the Garden of Eden man prayed, not with lip but with life, "Father, not *thy* will, but *mine* be done." God had made very clear his wish for the behavior of Adam and Eve. A time came, however, in which the desire of man and woman in Eden was at cross-purposes with the will of God; and, in this conflict of wills, they chose their way, not God's way. On the heels of Eden's prayer sin came into the world; and in its train came separation, suf-

23

fering, sorrow, heartache, and life-break—in short, all
the tragedies which sin has brought.

In the other garden, Gethsemane, the divine Son of
God literally prayed, "Father, if thou be willing, re-
move this cup from me: nevertheless not my will, but
thine, be done" (Luke 22:42). When personal preference and God's wisdom were in conflict, Christ chose
God's will. On the heels of that prayer came salvation
for men's souls, reconciliation to God, and the transformation of life. In short, Gethsemane's prayer
brought infinite good to all areas of human life.

Though those two gardens are far removed in time
from the day in which we live, we go into one of those
gardens at decision time in every instance in which our
wills are in conflict with the will of God. If the final
choice is *our* will instead of *God's* will, the decision is
a Garden of Eden decision. If the choice is to accept
God's clear will, despite possible great agony of spirit
in the consideration, we have made a Gethsemane decision.

I

The cost of Gethsemane's prayer to the person who
prays it is always greater at the moment; yet, in the
perspective of the years, it is very much better for the
individual who makes the decision, and infinitely better for his world, that he choose God's will instead of
his own will.

Look at the immediate cost to Jesus. Shortly after he
had prayed Gethsemane's prayer, he was seized by the

officers of his adversaries, dragged into a burlesque of a trial, humiliated in indescribable ways, and crucified with excruciating pain and sorrow. The cost was so bitter and high on that memorable day that there were, doubtless, many of his friends who questioned his wisdom in choosing Gethsemane's way.

Yet, today, the name of Christ is the most honored name on the horizon of our world. Throughout the world there are multiple millions of enlightened and intelligent people who live in his name, and even more millions who, though they do not follow him in faith, ascribe to his influence the credit for most of man's most significant advances in human welfare: education for the masses, healing for humanity's hurts, the widening emphasis upon the dignity of the individual and the sacredness of personality, the importance of little children, the elevation of womanhood, and the glorification of the family. These and innumerable other blessings have come to the world because of the teachings, spirit, and victory which Jesus brought to the world through Gethsemane's road. It was better for him and so much better for our world that he prayed the Gethsemane prayer!

On the other hand, praying Eden's prayer usually brings an initial gratification which may seem wonderfully sweet, immediately satisfying, and even measurably thrilling. The bitterness of Eden's way, however, comes eventually to be so vast that the individual cries out in remorse and despair; and, in addition to the tragedy which comes to the person who makes Eden's decision, there is a tragic outreach of that decision which hurts so many others now and later.

II

God's Word contains a large number of stark true-to-life stories of people who chose Eden's way. King Saul, first of Israel's kings, was in a particularly advantageous position to lead his people to obedience to God, because they had so much longed for a king. Saul knew God's will, for God revealed his will to him carefully through his prophet Samuel. Saul knew, for instance, that God had commanded that he and his army should destroy utterly the Amalekites and all of their property. Saul's preferences spoke out to contradict God's will, and he made the Eden decision. He yielded to vanity and brought King Agag back in captivity; he yielded to greed and brought back choice flocks and herds. A last glimpse of Saul's life reveals his beseeching a servant to hold a sword to facilitate the king's suicide.

Samson knew God's will in the matter of his marriage, for he had been so amply instructed by his righteous parents. When he found his preference at cross-purposes with God's will, he prayed Eden's prayer. Every reader of these lines will remember the dark tragedy of Samson's life thereafter: betrayed by his wife, his eyes put out, his strength put to doing an animal's work, and, in a display of his returned strength, his destruction of the pagan temple at the cost of his own life.

David, a man after God's own heart, knew so well the will of God concerning covetousness, lust, and adultery. In the same unwillingness to bring desires of the flesh into harmony with God's will, which was seen first in Eden, David consciously had his way instead of God's way, and the unhappy story of Bathsheba occurred in his life. The bitterness of Eden's decision also came to him, for no man in history has ever had a more sorrowful heart at the recognition of his own gross sins. Moreover, the revolt of his son Absalom and the denial of his great hope to build the Temple were dividends of Eden's prayer in David's life.

Jonah knew God's will so very clearly, but he determined to have his own way instead. Added to his obstinacy was his foolish thought that he could run away from God and inescapable duty. You will remember his ocean voyage, his being thrown overboard, his sojourn inside the great fish, his deliverance, and his later loss of joy in the belated doing of God's will. Eden's way had paid off in bitter coinage again!

God's Word contains, also, some happier episodes concerning people who did choose God's will instead of their own wills, when the two were in conflict. It would have been easier for Stephen, Christianity's first martyr after Christ, to heed the basic urge for self-preservation and to "hide his light under a bushel" through compromise and duplicity. Yet, in a very real translation of the Gethsemane spirit, he chose to follow God's will. With him, as with Christ, the initial cost was death; yet, the eventual result was immortality of the name, example, and influence of Stephen. An almost immediate result of his taking the Gethsemane road was the conversion of the man who had held the cloaks of the assassins who stoned Stephen to death, Paul himself!

From the moment of his facing Christ on the Damascus road, the continuing prayer of Paul's heart was, "Lord, what wilt thou have me to do?" (Acts 9:6) . The revelation of God's will dictated Paul's schedule and itinerary from that moment forward. Though there were many times thereafter in which he could have prayed Eden's prayer, he kept his heart filled with Gethsemane's prayer. Stonings, beatings, ostracism, shipwreck, imprisonment, and death were a part of the cost of that prayer to Paul. Today, however, his is one of the most honored names in Christian history, his example continues to stir millions to more heroic living, and the endless quality of his influence goes on through the ages. Paul's praying the Gethsemane prayer enriched Christianity greatly.

Luke prayed Gethsemane's prayer and became the beloved Christian physician. Zacchaeus turned from Eden's selfish way to Christ's Gethsemane way and became a redeemed, rectifying, Christian businessman. The woman at the well outside of Sychar had had her way in indulgence and self-gratification for so long that Eden's bitter cup had become her lot: she was unwanted at the well at the hours in which "decent" people came there. In her glorious experience with Christ at that well, she chose Gethsemane's way and became one of the first unofficial home missionaries in Christianity's history.

Matthew left his taxgathering, Peter left his lucrative fishing vocation, and other followers came in the Gethsemane spirit to permit God's will to transcend what might have been an easier way for them. That it was better for them and for subsequent ages that they came Gethsemane's way is so evident that we have barely to mention it.

III

So, the principles of Eden and Gethsemane come unchanged to you and me: in every instance in which our wills conflict with God's will, we must decide which of the two gardens we shall enter. The aftermath of the choice is unchanged, too: sacrifice immediately in the Gethsemane decision, but infinite joy and blessing later; sweetness and self-gratification immediately in the Eden decision, but bitterness to self and hurt to others in the after-years. Two very old gardens, but still the scene of the continuing effort of Satan to thwart the will of God for man!

With you and me the choice between Eden and Gethsemane may come in decisions from little to large, in areas from trite to tremendous. These decisions, furthermore, will have to be made as long as we live; for, as Paul wrote, "When I would do good, evil is present with me" (Rom. 7:21). Self will continue to cry out, and so frequently its demands will contradict the will of God. In principles of character and conduct, in all of our interpersonal relationships, in vocational choices, in choice of life mate and in conduct of marriage and home, in social and recreational activities, and in so many decisions related to these, we shall find that self's wish and God's will are often at cross purposes.

In choices in the arena of character and conduct we shall find that God's Word has offered completely adequate guidance concerning God's wish for the principles which determine character and result in conduct. Increasingly in our day the preferences of so many of our contemporaries and the more popular and profitable ways of life seem to lie in conflict with the clearly taught will of God for human conduct. To follow God's will may result in our appearing to our contemporaries to be naïve, queer, and "old fashioned." Regardless of the consequences, we shall be wise to make these vital decisions Gethsemane decisions.

In the choice of vocation, the individual's wish and God's will may be in conflict. Maximum success, fullest happiness, and largest contribution to society are at stake for the deciding individual; for, only when he is in harmony with the will of God for his vocation do these superlatives come to him. In the Gethsemane decision there is so often an immediate sacrifice necessitated, but Gethsemane's results are repeated over and over again today in the lives of individuals who come its way. Beyond the choice of *what* to do in vocation, there are two other vocational decisions: *where* to practice the vocation, and *how*—that is, in what spirit

—the lifework shall be done. There needs to be a surrendered willingness to go anywhere God directs, and the vocation needs to be practiced in such a spirit of unselfish humility that it brings glory to Christ.

With distressing frequency young people are tempted to make Samson's choice in marriage; they are tempted to go against all the wisdom of God's Word and against the wise counsel of family and friends. All who follow Samson into Eden for this choice will find their own version of Eden's eventual bitterness in marriages which never achieve the happiness that God intended, marriages which tend to break up under the tensions which unwise decisions always bring. In addition to the decision of *whom* to marry, there is the important decision of *when* to marry. Many young people choose their way instead of God's way and rush into marriage before achieving adequate maturity and preparation.

In the conduct of marriage and family, the decision must be made concerning what principles shall govern. In the wisdom of an Old Testament stalwart, many couples decide at the outset, "As for me and my house, we will serve the Lord" (Josh. 24:15). Others are Eden-praying couples who take the easy and popular road of doing whatever is the popular thing, permitting their children to do likewise. Eden's fruits of that sort of marriage and family litter the American scene with many tragic tokens: broken homes, juvenile delinquency, children robbed of the heritage of happiness and normalcy.

There is no more crucial area of Christian decision in our day than that denoted by the words "social and recreational life." A large sector of Christianity in our land has lost its distinctiveness: it no longer hears or obeys the unmistakable call of both the Old Testament and the New Testament, "Come out from among them, and be ye separate" (2 Cor. 6:17).

Many Christians are driven by a compelling fear that their contemporaries will not like them if they are truly spiritual in their social and recreational lives— an almost amazing fear of being thought to be "Victorian" or "outmoded." Many Christians go to nearly incredible lengths in order to win social position or preference, identifying themselves completely with the social compromises and sins of our times. There is small wonder that there are not continuing conversions of great throngs of people when we hear that a recently converted man attributes his greatest encouragement to continue in his dissolute practices of drinking and gambling to the examples of Christians and church members who were doing the same things! The need to make Gethsemane decisions concerning social and recreational activities in our day is increasingly urgent for Christians of all ages.

IV

The Christians who continue to bless our society most with their efforts and with the impact of their influence are those who have come to their present spiritual status through the Gethsemane way. Some of these Christians are men and women whose names and influence are well known. Others of them are in unglamorous places, whose decisions and influence are not heralded in news media, but whose Gethsemane-made decisions touch with determining influence the lives of individuals, groups, and institutions.

Albert Schweitzer, universally known, admired, and honored, came to a time in which he knew that God's way led to his becoming a medical missioner to Africa. Had he listened to Eden's beckonings, he could have taught with distinction in European universities, for he was brilliantly prepared in philosophy; he could have filled the most excellent pulpits, for he was marvelously trained in theology; he could have made a fabulous fortune in playing Bach's music on organs around the world, for he was widely regarded as a magnificent organist. Eden's way would have brought material comforts, financial remuneration, and no end of plaudits from his day.

Gethsemane's way necessitated Schweitzer's going to medical college after all of his other brilliant preparations had been concluded. His decision called upon him to relinquish all hope of comfort, convenience, and immediate fame. Furthermore, there was the imminent possibility that some associates of that time would consider him to be a stark fool! But, already in his lifetime, Schweitzer's decision has become a blessing of such magnitude that the entire world stands in deference to him. Only the endless years of eternity can prove the vastness of the wisdom of his decision.

There are many other inspiring episodes of the Gethsemane road in our time: Dr. Wilfred Grenfell's departure for the barren wastes of Labrador, when he might have luxuriated in London's Mayfair with comfort, convenience, and tremendous income. . . . The departures each month for foreign mission service of brilliant young physicians who, had they prayed Eden's prayer, would never have gone. . . . The heroic decisions every year of magnificent young people to give their lives to selfless service at home and abroad. . . . The growing number of people in all vocations who follow the example of the young doctor who responds to inquiries concerning the nature of his work by saying, "I am a Christian doctor," meaning that Christ stands first in his thinking and planning. . . . The example of the doctor on whose waiting room wall there was a plaque for all to see: *Christ first, others second.* . . . The increasing number of proprietors of businesses who forego profits which alcoholic beverages would bring, because the Gethsemane way does not permit profits from such sources. . . . And the little-known ones in humble niches who, in their own wonderful ways, pray daily, "not my will, but thine be done."

To which of these gardens have you gone so often that a well-beaten path is there—Eden or Gethsemane?

4. Two Prayers

And he spake this parable unto certain which trusted in themselves that they were righteous, and despised others: Two men went up into the temple to pray; the one a Pharisee, and the other a publican. The Pharisee stood and prayed thus with himself, God, I thank thee, that I am not as other men are, extortioners, unjust, adulterers, or even as this publican. I fast twice in the week, I give tithes of all that I possess. And the publican, standing afar off, would not lift up so much as his eyes unto heaven, but smote upon his breast, saying, God, be merciful to me a sinner. I tell you, this man went down to his house justified rather than the other.

LUKE 18:9–14

ONE DOES NOT HAVE TO BE A PSYCHOLogist to discern some things concerning character traits of other people. For instance, one can listen discerningly over a period of time to the praying of people in religious groups and sense some indications of spiritual status: humility or vanity, sincerity or bombast, vitality or lethargy, altruism or selfishness, surrender or conceit.

It was so with the prayers of the two men in Luke 18:9–14. The Pharisee's prayer revealed a pompous spirit, pride which had grown to proportions of vanity and arrogance, and an evident yearning for publicity of his self-appraised virtues. His prayer is painful to read or hear. As a spiritual exercise, it was surely powerless. Christ aptly described the Pharisee as being among those "which trusted in themselves that they were righteous, and despised others." It would have been better for his fellow man and for the cause of religion had he stayed at home. His prayer offended God, it cast aspersions upon his fellow man, and it brought power to nobody.

The publican, on the other hand, prayed a simple prayer which may be well described as *plain, pertinent, personal,* and *prevailing.* If he had virtues and religious achievements, he evidently felt that they were insignificant in the presence of the great God to whom he was praying. He was overwhelmed by his own imperfections and was keenly conscious of his need for forgiveness from his merciful God. His prayer revealed humility of spirit, sincerity of purpose, devotion to the God of righteousness. His prayer received the approval of Jesus, who said, "I tell you, this man went down to his house justified rather than the other."

In both public and private praying, we, too, reveal much concerning our inner selves and concerning our relationships to God and man. A frank personal examination of our praying will reveal, perhaps shockingly, how much we lean in the direction of the Pharisee, and how little we reflect the contrite, humble spirit of the publican. What are some of the things which our praying may reveal?

I

First, our praying may reveal much about our relationship to God. Our prayers may reveal the state of the *vitality* of that relationship. This revelation may come in the very spirit of the prayer. If the relationship is stale—no real growth in our understanding of God, of his will for our lives, of his passion for reconciling our world, or no improvement in our obedience toward the expectations of God—our prayers are likely to carry a sameness, if not a staleness, which does not change with the years. However, if the relationship is warm, intimate, and growing in power and obedience, there will be a vital freshness in our praying, indicating growth, discovery, devotion, and enthusiasm.

Also revealed in our praying will be the degree of *honesty* maintained between ourselves and God. That degree of honesty is likely to be indicated by the candor and sorrow with which we confess our sins, by the degree of sincerity in which we talk to God about our personal plans and problems, and by the eagerness with which we thank God for the blessings which the average person either takes for granted or presumes to be his rightful dividend. If our lives are filled with duplicity, disobedience, or selfishness, our prayers will be filled with mere words but little spirit; and the words themselves will indicate that, knowing that we can deceive neither God nor ourselves, we are trying to deceive our hearers!

The degree of *surrender to God's will* present in our individual lives will also be revealed in our praying. If there is deep, permeating, abiding obedience in our lives, our prayers will be characterized by a simplicity of language, by a humility of attitude, and by a warmth of heart which complete surrender brings. If, however, we are not walking in a state of obedience toward God, our praying is likely to be marked by much verbiage, by the use of lofty but nonpersonal terminology, and by the absence of any real commitments. We may even sound as if we were delivering an address to a distant, lofty stranger; or we may appear to be tossing compliments toward a God whom we secretly fear but whom we do not obey. There will be missing from our prayers the melody of a life in harmony with the will of God.

Our prayers may reveal, too, the nature of the *fear* of our hearts toward God. The fear element in praying may indicate an almost superstitious attitude toward God—almost the attitude of the pagan who fears that if he does not pray, his deity will punish him. Such prayer becomes, not the supplication of a devoted child, but an attempt to placate or "buy off" the wrath of God. Or the fear indicated may be the fear of Bible-promised punishment from God for unholy acts of life, which acts the Christian does not mean to relinquish short of dire tragedy.

On the other hand, our prayers may indicate the sort of wholesome fear which is appropriate in the life of any child of God: the fear, born of a tremendous love and devotion, which causes one to want to be sure not to do anything which will bring sorrow to the object of so great a love. This kind of fear in a Christian's prayers is happily contagious and is likely to touch hearers' hearts with resolution, born of love, not to offend God.

II

In the second place, our prayers may indicate much about our relationships to fellow man. The self-righteousness of the Pharisee, so disgustingly demonstrated in his prayer, indicated both a sense of superiority toward his fellow man and the absence of any feeling of responsibility toward the well-being of others. More than that, according to the Scripture passage, there was evidently a sort of contempt in his heart for the publican. Our prayers, too, may indicate a complete disinterest in the well-being of others or a deliberate ignoring of our obligations to those about us, or, worse still, an essential disdain for others. In so praying we reveal that we are but contemporary counterparts of the scribes and Pharisees, whom Jesus so soundly denounced.

In a graphically challenging sermon from his pulpit in Little Rock, Arkansas, Dr. Dale Cowling spoke forcefully of the scribes and Pharisees of Jesus' time. He pointed out that theirs was a "religion for religion's sake" and asserted that it was a "bigoted, narrow-minded, self-centered kind of religion." He said further, "This kind of religion has always been the greatest threat to Christianity: its followers robed themselves in self-righteousness and murdered the Son of God on Calvary's cross." [1]

Does your praying reveal something of the pharasaical attitude toward your fellow man? If the attitude is in our hearts, it will surely creep into our prayers, and discerning listeners can detect it!

On the other hand, the Christian's prayers may indicate toward fellow man a sense of humble gratitude, a sense of compassionate love and sympathy, a sense of yearning to reach out to help. The very spirit of such prayers reveals that the Christian has walked and talked with his fellow man, listening to his hopes, lifting his loads, binding up his wounds, sharing his sorrows, touching others with the balm of Christian love. The very proportion of the Christian's prayers given to a sense of concern for the well-being of mankind around the world will indicate the proportion of his thinking given to the needs of his fellow man.

Many people throughout one of our southern states remember with gratitude a magnificent woman whose praying reflected her living in regard to service to people about her. She had every opportunity to become selfish and self-centered. She had money, education, position, a wonderfully happy marriage, joy in her husband's success, gratification in the superb behavior of her children. When she prayed, she prayed with the needs of mankind pressing upon her heart, yearning in her spirit to help in alleviating those needs. A peep into any one day of her life revealed that she strove constantly to meet as many of those needs as possible. As she lived, so she prayed: her warm compassion for others was revealed in her praying!

In another state many will remember the prayers of a leading minister: they were so full of heartbeat that tears of compassion frequently accompanied his praying. Those who knew him were aware that he merely prayed as he lived, for he carried the heartaches of a whole city in his heart and expended his energies to the limit in seeking to alleviate the needs of others.

III

In the third place, our prayers may well indicate the degree of spiritual maturity to which we have proceeded. The discerning listener can tell whether or not we are shallow in our spiritual thinking and acting on the basis of whether or not we get to the very roots of the matters about which we pray. He can tell, further, whether or not we are childish or mature on the basis of the requests which we make for ourselves and for others, and on the basis of the roles which we assign to both ourselves and God in bringing our wishes to pass.

Some Christians pray with requests to God which are as childish as a seven-year-old's asking his father urgently for a motorcycle. Others pray as if God were an errand boy to do their chores, or an indulgent Santa Claus to hear and honor their slightest requests. It is normal for children to have the "give me" complex in their praying, but the mature Christian's praying should have more of the "use me" spirit when he is asking God to bring desirable things to pass.

The mature Christian's prayers will surely indicate that he has grown in faith, in his hold upon God's Word, in his understanding of God's plans and purposes, in unselfishness of spirit, in the mature grace of patience, in his capacity to bear heavy loads, in his willingness to share the loads of others, in his growing sense of unworthiness of God's love and grace, in a growing desire to practice the mature challenges of Christianity in love and forgiveness, and in willingness to do the will of God, regardless of cost.

A wonderful layman often reveals his maturity in Christian love and forgiveness and, at the same time, inspires hearers to resolve to grow toward maturity in this important area by praying, "Forgive us our sins, *as we have already forgiven those who have sinned against us."* That simple prayer speaks volumes about that layman's spiritual maturity! A college student, mature beyond his years in spiritual insight and power, so revealed his maturity of understanding of God and man that fellow students remarked, "His prayers always leave us with the desire to move up to a higher level of Christian living." A quiet woman who prayed occasionally in the prayer meetings of her church prayed with such mature insight and power that her hearers had the feeling of being virtually in the kindergarten of spiritual development! Mature praying *does* reveal mature living.

IV

Our praying may well reveal, too, the scope of our concern for the fulfilment of the Great Commission. The normal prayer of the little child has much of its own wishes and whims and usually reaches out only to those who contribute to its well-being and happiness. The normal prayer of the mature Christian will reveal much concern for the whole world, for the plight of men who do not know Jesus, for the awakening of fellow Christians to a vital relationship to world missions. Our praying will, therefore, reveal whether we are provincial or worldwide in our concern for lost people, whether we are theoretical or personal in our relationship to the Great Commission, whether we are casual or fervent in our sense of concern for the preaching of the gospel around the world.

You have heard the prayers of people, doubtless, in whose prayers you felt the throbbing movement of hearts which love lost people. People who pray such prayers are doing something about the Great Commission on the home front; they are sustaining in love and prayer those who are taking the message of Christ throughout the world. Then, perhaps, you have heard other prayers which mentioned the spreading of the gospel in a perfunctory, nonpersonal sense, but from which prayers was missing any evidence that the makers of those prayers had done anything personally to facilitate the fulfilment of the Great Commission.

V

In the final analysis, if one's praying is to improve, one's *living* will need to improve. "Getting out of the shallows" in praying will have to be preceded by the Christian's "launching out into the deep" in his spiritual growth. The prayers of the Pharisee and the publican merely mirrored the spiritual status of two people. The Pharisee's prayer was unacceptable because his life was characterized by wrong attitudes. The publican's prayer was acceptable because the spiritual attitude of the man who prayed was honest, seeking, growing. As each lived, so he prayed, the prayer life of each revealing his daily living.

Proceeding on the basis of seeking the *cause* for a *result* which has impressed us, we can study prayer itself to great spiritual advantage. First, we can study closely the prayers recorded in the Bible, prayers prayed by individuals whose lives, also, are recorded there. The relationship between their living and their praying provides an interesting study. These prayers will include prayers of many Old Testament stalwarts, including supplications for guidance, for power, for victory, for forgiveness of sin, and prayers in behalf of others. This prayer study will include also the New Testament prayers, including the fervent prayer-times of Christ, of his disciples, and of the apostle Paul. The Christian who desires urgently to grow in life-power and prayer-power could spend devotional periods of many weeks in this study to great advantage.

Second, we can study the prayers of great Christians down through the ages to discern both *how* they prayed and *why* they prayed as they did. The prayers of many saints and seers, heroes and martyrs have been preserved in literature and in religious writings. A study of these prayers could significantly enrich our understanding and appreciation of prayer. In addition to a study of the foregoing prayers, we may well peruse such little volumes as Baillie's *A Diary of Private Prayer,*[2] and Head's *He Sent Leanness.*[3] These will both stimulate and sting, but they will surely call our attention helpfully to the weaknesses of our praying and to the lives which make such praying inevitable.

Third, we can read books on prayer. There are many helpful books on library and religious book store shelves which deal exclusively with developing power in prayer. The Christian would be blessed through reading at least one of these books each year.

Finally, we can improve our prayer lives through developing better prayer habits. Praying regularly at an appointed time and in a conducive place, praying aloud when alone, praying at regular times with prayer partners, keeping a prayer list—objects to be prayed for and answered prayers to be thankful for—these are some habits which help.

But let us remember forever that the greatest improvement in our praying will come from the greatest improvement in our living; that the closer we walk in fellowship with Christ, the finer our praying will be. Our prayer lives will not move from the Pharisee-type to the publican-type—from offensive to acceptable—until our personal daily living has moved from self-indulgence and self-satisfaction to Christ indwelling and Christ-control!

PART TWO

Three Lights

Three Who Passed By

Three Crosses

Three Calls for Tears

In Which
The Christian Is Challenged to
Proceed toward Maturity in
Stewardship of Talent Within
His Church, in Christian Service
Outside His Church, in A Better
Concept of Cross-Bearing, and
in The Art of a Mature Accept-
ance of What Life Brings

5. Three Lights

And God made two great lights; the greater light to rule the day, and the lesser light to rule the night: he made the stars also. GENESIS 1:16

IN THE TERSE AND DESCRIPTIVE MANner in which Genesis presents the thrilling drama of creation, the creation and mission of the sun, moon, and stars are related in one brief verse. The writer made no attempt to give an astronomer's detailed explanation of the relation of these heavenly bodies to the remainder of the universe, but went straight to the point of indicating their light-giving responsibilities to our earth.

It is evident from this poignant verse that the three levels of light described were created with varying powers for different purposes insofar as giving light to planet earth is concerned, and that each of these levels of light is expected to perform its light-giving function in keeping with its capacity. The function of the sun in giving light to our earth, for instance, is much greater than the light-giving function assigned to the moon;

yet, it matters significantly that both lights perform according to individual capacities to fulfil the light-giving mission assigned.

What if the Creator had committed to these heavenly bodies the freedom of choice and action with which man is endowed, and what if one of these heavenly bodies, of its own volition and apart from the will of God, could and should decide to tailor down its contribution of light to our earth? Suppose, for instance, the sun could and should reduce its contribution of light to our earth? We know that dire results would ensue, for much of the earth's energy has always come from the sun. It matters that the sun live up to its candle power!

Or what if the moon could and should tailor down its light contribution to planet earth (for reasons as unacceptable as man so often uses in not living up to his candle power!)? Though we cannot anticipate all of the results of such action, we know that the results would be drastic. Although, in giving light to our earth, the moon is a lesser light, it matters urgently that it live up to its candle power.

"And the stars, also!" It is entirely probable that the writer of Genesis 1:16 meant to include in the word *stars* the other heavenly bodies, even the ones which we call planets, for their light-giving to our earth is, like that of the stars, less than the light contribution of the sun and moon. Insofar as giving light to planet earth is concerned, the contribution of these stars seems quite small to the nonscientific observer; yet, we know that God's plan for his universe needs every one of the stars, even the ones which, because of their remoteness, seem so small to us. Therefore, if it were possible for a star, apart from the will of God, to cease to shine, it is only reasonable to say that the delicate balance of God's universe would be disturbed, and that his plan would be incomplete. Small though some of the stars may seem to you and me, it matters greatly that each star live up to its candle power.

Now, let us look quickly into the parable of talents in Matthew 25:14–30 for a stimulating parallel. To his servants the departing lord gave talents according to their varying abilities: to one man he gave five talents, to another he gave two, and to a third he gave one talent. The parallel is interesting: *greater light, lesser light, "stars also"; five talents, two talents, one talent.*

Upon his return, the lord called for an accounting. The greater light, the five-talented man, had evidently developed the talents left with him and had used them in ways which brought credit to the lord who had entrusted them to him. Therefore, there had happened what always happens to talents so handled: they had doubled in worth, and the five-talented man now had ten talents. Splendid commendation came to him from his lord, the stress being upon the faithfulness with which he had handled his talents.

The two-talented man, a lesser light, had less in quantity than his predecessor, but he had been just as faithful in the development and lord-honoring use of his talents. Therefore, he brought four talents and was

given the identical commendation which the greater
light had received; for he, too, had lived up to his candle power.

The one-talented man not only had not developed,
used, and shared his talent but had buried it in the
earth! His excuse, pathetically indicative of his lack of
appreciation and concern for good stewardship of the
talent left with him by his lord, evoked both a scathing
reproof and a drastic action on the part of the lord. He
was called "Thou wicked and slothful servant," and the
talent was taken from him to be given to one of his fel-
lows who had proved that he knew what to do with talents. The attitude of Christ toward Christians who
do not live up to their candle power was made abun-
dantly clear through the denunciation and action recorded in this parable.

With God-created lights and with God-created people it is unmistakably evident that the Creator expects
his creations to live up to individual candle power, and
to perform according to capacities committed. It is
clear that God expects every individual to develop his
God-given talents, to use them constructively and cre-
atively, and to share those talents with the God who
gave them by using them in ways which reflect honor
upon him and in ways which facilitate the coming of
the kingdom of God on our earth. The thing which
matters most is not how much light power or talent
power the individual possesses; rather, the great determinant of God's pleasure or displeasure toward us is
whether or not we live up to the amount of power

entrusted to us individually. It matters greatly to God that you and I live up to our candle power!

Though the development of abilities through study and preparation is worthy of many chapters of discussion, and though the constructive and creative use of these abilities merits other chapters, we shall confine our discussion here to the Christian's use of his talents in witnessing and serving. It is only logical that the Christian give back to God a portion of the fruits of his developed talents; for, it must be remembered, what he has done in study and development of these abilities would be worthless had God not given him the capacities originally.

I

Are you a five-talented Christian? Are you living up to your candle power in witnessing and serving? Or are you, perchance, determining the amount of your contribution on the basis of such erroneous standards as "I'm already doing more than anyone else in my church," or "I am willing, but I shall wait until I am asked"? As we readily recognize, the five-talented man in the parable could have used only three of his talents and have been doing more than anyone else in the group. We know, too, that in the eyes of his lord he would have been performing at only sixty per cent of his capacity, and that he would not have received the glorious commendation which came to him.

If you are one of God's greater lights and are not actually living up to your candle power in the matter of sharing your abilities in witnessing and serving, primarily through your church, I wonder if you know the threefold blessing which is being missed?

First, *you* are missing the tremendous blessing which the sense of joy in your own heart would bring. The sense of knowing that you have been a good steward of God-given abilities would make your fellowship with God a warm, smiling, joyous blessing. The knowledge that, through a complete sharing of your abilities in Christian witnessing and serving, you are facilitating the world's most important enterprise, the fulfilment of the Great Commission, would bring you joy. Too, the knowledge that the use of those God-given abilities had helped to strengthen others spiritually would bring to your heart a sense of gratification.

Second, *God* is missing the joy for which his heart yearns. The great, compelling hope of God's heart is that the world be reconciled to him through Christ. His love for our world once impelled him to send his choicest gift, his only begotten Son. Your performing to the limit of your abilities automatically strengthens the work of the church and the outreach of its main mission of winning men to God. Therefore, your life becomes an asset to Christ, to his church, and to the all-important task of reconciling men to God. Your failure to live up to your candle power robs God's heart of great joy.

Third, *others* are missing the inspiration of the dedicated example of a talented life if you are not doing your best in witnessing and serving. Because you are a greater light in ability, the impact of your humble, happy dedication of those abilities to Christian service and witnessing "packs an extra punch," inspiring other multi-talented Christians and even less-talented ones to begin to do their best. Since you are probably a successful person in your career, or you are an outstanding leader in high school or college, the fact that you find or "make" time for full participation in the ministry of your church carries a sermon on stewardship of ability more powerful than any sermon on that subject which your pastor may deliver from the pulpit. Thereby you do bring inspiration, strength, and joy to others in living up to your candle power.

Two eminent professional men were members of the same church. Both were five-talented men. One was an active deacon, a leader in youth work, a participant in the music program of the church, and a faithful helper in visitation and witnessing. Though he was frequently called out of services for emergency calls, his faithfulness in attendance was inspiring. He went to great pains to make the full range of his ability available to his church.

The second man, though a man of irreproachable character, was making no worthwhile contribution to his church. He held no office, he performed no service, he carried no part of the load of the program within the church nor in its program of reaching out into the community. He had even persuaded himself to the conclusion that he was too busy to attend church meetings regularly. His life was barren of the joys which living up to his candle power would have brought: he was denying his God, his church, and his fellow Christians the inspiration and blessing which better stewardship of his gifted life would have brought. Despite his excellent moral character, he was a "wicked and slothful servant" in his Lord's sight.

II

Or are you, perhaps, a lesser light, a two-talented person? You would love to do solos in the choir, but you know that there are other voices better suited to solos than yours; therefore, you sing with radiance and faithfulness in the chorus. Or you would love to be president of a group, teacher of a class, superintendent of a department, or director of some organization; yet, knowing that there are others who can do the job better, you accept a subordinate responsibility with happiness and good stewardship. In short, you play "second fiddle" with the best you have!

What would our choruses be with only solo voices? What would our orchestras be without their second instruments? What would drama be if there were no supporting characters? The choruses and orchestras would lack depth, range, and appeal; drama would lose some of its most lovable and memorable characters. Subordinate and supporting roles are indispensable to music, drama, and life!

In Christian service, some of the most valuable and Christlike participants through the centuries have been the lesser lights—people who have performed with love and devotion to the limit of their lesser abilities, never asking for the spotlight, never waiting to be publicized and praised, never stopping to demand gratitude. Many of these two-talented people have demonstrated more Christian grace and spirit than their more talented associates; for, as Spurgeon once said, "It takes more grace than I can tell, to play the second fiddle well."

III

But if you are, honestly, a one-talented person, an "also" of the light creation, it matters so much that you, too, shall give your best in witnessing and serving, however small your best may be. If you have been thinking that your contribution to your church and to the fulfilment of the Great Commission is so small that it does not matter that you make it, or that your contribution is so small that it would not be missed, let us point out some ways in which you can contribute significantly.

Lest someone dismiss these ways as being insignificant, let it be said with emphasis that if they constitute *all* the contribution possible for you to make, they will be honored of God and warmly appreciated by your church. Instead of complaining that you cannot preach or teach or preside or sing or conduct or direct, why not search for the lesser things which you can do, and do them with all your power?

For instance, you can *attend* with such faithfulness that your name will be mentioned among those who can be counted upon to be present, regardless of the difficult circumstances. As the post office department's motto says, "Neither snow nor rain nor heat nor gloom of night shall stay these couriers from the swift completion of their appointed rounds," your church will say, "Nothing short of the impossible will keep him (or her) away, and we are not sure that the impossible will!"

You can *listen* with such radiant attention that those who do preach or teach or sing will find in your devoted listening a source of inspiration to them to do their best.

You can *pray* for those who will be in leadership, both prior to their hours of performance and during their times of service. Often those in leadership will attest, "There was power available to me today for which I could not personally account." You and God will know whence came that power.

You can *invite* people with such radiance and constancy that some will attend whose lives may receive enrichment, even transformation. God will remember that those persons would not even have been present to receive such blessings if you had not done your significant bit to get them to God's house.

You can *smile* with the love of God behind your smile, so that people's hearts will be blessed by the radiant happiness of your face; and surely some will say, "That person's smile just does fine things to my heart." Your dedicated smile, though a simple thing, will have pointed people to Jesus.

Little things? They are not little things if they constitute the maximum talent of a Christian; and God will bless the giver of these apparently minor contributions with great joy and usefulness for living up to his candle power. In many churches, and other institutions throughout America, some of the most inspiring people are those dear ones whose talents are tiny, whose capacity for witnessing and serving is so much smaller than that of the greater and the lesser lights, but who glow to the limit of their candle power.

Thousands of alumni of a Southern university remember with affection a janitor whose labors of love to the limit of his ability were immortalized at his death by a bronze marker on the campus. Thousands of readers of newspapers in the spring of 1960 were thrilled by an account of a custodian in a school: his completely·on-the-altar life of service brought to him such love and gratitude that the 1960 school yearbook was dedicated to him. Many will recall the devotion of a large church to a girl whose life was limited in more ways than one, but whose complete devotion to her church won such love that at her funeral the flowers and attendance matched similar tributes paid at times of death of the city's leading citizens. The quiet, faithful, listening, praying, loving ones who strengthen thousands of churches with humility and goodness have brought a legacy of great inspiration and strength.

Have you ever seen a star through a telescope? It is the most beautiful of all the heavenly lights. God looks at the "little" people through the telescope of love and truth, and they are beautiful beyond description—

most of all, because, despite their littleness of size and scope, they are living up to their candle power!

Regardless of the level at which you appear in the galaxy of lights or in the range of ability, are *you* living up to your candle power?

6. Three Who Passed By

LUKE 10:30–35

IN THE AMAZING TERSENESS WITH
which he told his never-to-be-forgotten parables, Jesus
told the story of the good Samaritan. You will remember the situation: a man left stripped and wounded by
robbers on a roadside, the coming and passing of two
official representatives of religion, and the coming of
the lowly Samaritan with compassion and action in
binding up the man's wounds. In six little verses Jesus
gave one of the most dramatic episodes of reaction to
human need ever presented!

First of all, a priest passed by the man who had been
robbed, wounded, and left in a half-dead condition.
The record indicates that this high official of organized
religion not only did not pause, he "passed by on the
other side." It taxes one's imagination to figure out this
apparently calloused attitude on the part of any child
of God; but it seems positively incredible that a man
dedicated to religious work would not have responded
with compassion and help in a time of such evident and

pressing need. Why did the priest pass by without even a look of sympathy?

Could it be that he just did not care? Could it be that he was on such a "tight schedule" and so wrapped up in the administrative duties which were his that he excused himself in the light of his busy schedule? Could it be that this sort of problem had not been assigned to him and, therefore, he felt no responsibility for helping? Could it be that he was just selfish, self-centered, indifferent, intolerant, prejudiced? Could it be that the remoteness of the situation from the eyes of men or that no one would see him performing an act of helpfulness removed the desire to help? Why . . . Why . . . Why?

Regardless of the reason for his lack of care or compassion, his action was reprehensible and won the evident disapproval of the compassionate Jesus. While people of that day did not see his failure and did not reprove this religionist for his lack of practicing the compassion which he had preached, God did see, and Jesus did record his unfortunate behavior for all succeeding ages to read and reprove. Let us hope that the priest was haunted by conscience and memory for days thereafter and that his reaction to human need improved on later occasions.

Secondly, there passed by a Levite. He did improve a bit upon the behavior of the priest, for he came and looked upon the wounded man with some degree of interest and sympathy; but that was the limit of his compassion, for he, too, passed by on the other side.

There may have been a fleeting sense of desire to help and a faint sense that he ought to help. Yet, he, too, was evidently so immersed in his own plans, or perhaps so preoccupied with a "tremendous load" of religious duties that he went along without helping. He may even have hoped that someone else with less religious responsibility and more time would come by later. To all practical purposes, however, he left the man to die. How could he have enjoyed his religious duties for the days ahead, unless conscience had ceased to remind him of human need unmet?

Though but two short verses are used to relate the coming and the action of the third passer-by, a Samaritan, those verses present an eloquent episode of love in action. He came, he saw, he felt compassion; he helped. Then, instead of feeling that he had done his part and that some later traveler should befriend the wounded man with a lift, he took him to an inn and looked after him overnight. Upon departing, he paid the host and promised to pay later for any subsequent expenses incident to the wounded man's recovery.

This lowly Samaritan, a man of a mixed race which was despised by the devout Jews of that day, had out-loved, outserved, and outlived even the official representatives of the established religion of his day and area! He may not have had time to stop and help, but he took time. He did not have the obligation to help perhaps, but he assumed the obligation with warm compassion. He wanted to help, because of a compassionate heart. Despite his lowly status, he had given a glorious demonstration of the love of God in meeting human need.

I

Though the circumstances and cast of characters may be different today, all of us are traveling the Jericho road constantly. There are people all about us who have been robbed—sometimes by circumstances beyond their control, sometimes by their own folly, and at other times by the follies of other people. These roadside victims have been deeply wounded by the impact of their experiences, and some of them are very really half-dead with discouragement, defeat, or sin. Past them every day go great throngs of Christians. Among these passers-by are some wonderful counterparts of the gracious Samaritan; but, alack and alas, even among today's followers of Jesus there are also counterparts of the priest and the Levite. Let us look at some contemporary situations which are in point.

There are people all about us whose lives have been robbed and wounded by sin. Yes, they knew all along that they were sinning and that the eventual penalty would bring sorrow and tragedy. Now the inevitable has come: the sinner is faced with shame, loss, and penalty. There he lies on today's Jericho road, and here come the passers-by.

The modern-day priest not only does not stop to help, but he is so fearful that somebody will connect him with the sin-wounded casualty that he looks the other way and passes rapidly by. In his heart are perhaps such mutterings as, "He made his own bed; now let him lie in it. . . . It serves him right; he had it coming to him; why should I soil my hands with his self-inflicted difficulties?" Or, if accompanied by another of his kind, today's counterpart of the priest would, doubtless, throw these and other stones of audible criticism at the wounded person. Also, it just may be that this "Christian" has much work to do on a talk for some religious group concerning the love of God!

Today's Levite comes along, too. He is sorry that the roadside victim is in such unfortunate condition. He even wishes that it had not happened. He may even mutter a few words of sympathy without slowing down to a full pause, lest he be asked to help. "After all," he muses, "it's not my responsibility to mend the broken pieces of society. Let the preachers and social workers look after people like this." He, too, moves on to some meeting, perhaps in which he may even speak eloquently of meeting society's needs through the church!

But sooner or later, thank God, today's Samaritan comes along. Like the original Samaritan, he is not necessarily a prominent person; he may even be of lowly social or racial classification; yet, he has been with Jesus and has learned to respond to humanity's hurts with a heart full of love. He asks no questions of the wounded ones, he seeks no compensation and praise, he loses no time. He sees a need which compassionate Christianity ought to meet and he goes to work to meet that need.

Today's Samaritan may have had little or no psychology and sociology to equip him for helping "maladjusted individuals," but he has love, sympathy, tenderness, patience, faith, and hope. Armed with these, he lends a hand to the sin-broken life. He saves his preaching and reproof for later, because this tragic one needs healing of heart and life first; later, in the spirit of Jesus, today's Samaritan can urge the sin-hurt individual to go his way and sin no more.

The Samaritan goes out of his way, at cost to himself, even at the risk of his own reputation at the hands of the self-righteous. But his is the way in which sinners are loved into the experience of regeneration and forgiveness. And, being no public speaker, he probably does not have a chance to tell vast audiences of his compassionate performances!

II

In addition to the sin-smitten people on the Jericho road there are so many others whose lives need the touch of compassion which Jesus wants his followers to give. There are the sick, the invalid, the sorrowing, the problem-pressed people of our day. The passers-by see them, too, and their reactions will normally follow the patterns of either the priest, the Levite, or the Samaritan.

The priest sees, judges, and passes on quickly. "These things come to all of us; so, why should that person expect to be exempt? Everybody has hard luck. It can be the making of the man. Let him shoulder his own load; everybody else has enough to worry about. What's more, I am one of the busiest church workers of this city. I do my part in other ways. This is no responsibility of mine." And on he goes to the empty, pompous duties which a mere machine could do, since compassion is not required. He is not only a debit to Christianity, but he is a positive reproach to it.

The Levite, too, comes along in a great hurry to get to compassionless duties. He pauses, feels a fleeting sense of compassion, but remembers that he has too much to do to be interrupted at this time. "I surely am sorry for the poor chap," he opines. "I hope that some one of the officials or agencies will look after him. He's in a bad way, but I suppose he has friends who will look after him." The inescapable words of Paul, "Bear ye one another's burdens, and so fulfil the law of Christ" (Gal. 6:2), seem to have made no impression upon this Levite. Or perhaps he interprets the "ye" in the passage as referring to the nonofficial constituency of Christianity, surely not to people in leadership who are as busy as he!

How glad we are that there are contemporary "good Samaritans" among the passers-by! Here comes one now: his heart is touched immediately and deeply by the sickness, by the invalid's couch or chair, by the weary and the heavy-laden, by the sorrowing, and by the problem-pressed pilgrims along the way. He does not pause to ask *why* the person is in this state of need or despair; he does not attempt to judge, for that is not his role. He simply knows that here is a need for compassionate understanding and urgent burden-bearing of another's load; and in that spirit he gives himself immediately and unselfishly to pouring on the oil of compassionate love, sympathy, and help.

This wonderful Christian binds up as many wounds in people's lives as possible, his only regret being his inability to do more for their wounded or broken lives. His love-impelled smile, his heartfelt sympathy, his tender assistance, his patient listening, his compassionate tears, his strengthening prayers leave many of life's victims with new hopes and rekindled joys. And, when he has done his best, he tries to leave these wounded ones in connection with others who can help. The priest and the Levite are not worthy to make religious talks in any group in which this Samaritan sits!

III

As you and God know your life, which one of the three passers-by do you most resemble? Do you remember with wincing shame some times in which you know that you acted the role of the priest or the Levite? Do you remember some times in which, though you did not have time, you took time to act in the spirit of the good Samaritan? Do you recall the warm sense of joy and nearness to Jesus which you felt when you displayed his compassionate spirit toward human need along the way?

Regardless of what your past reaction to human frailty and human need has been, why not become a consistent good Samaritan? There is a great shortage, you know. How greatly the prestige of Christianity will go up when a Christian takes time to ease humanity's hurts in the good Samaritan spirit!

Would some pointers in developing the good Samaritan's spirit be helpful? We shall discover and develop many other attitudes, techniques, and capacities, once we have begun seriously to follow our Master's spirit toward people in need. Here are a few "starters" with which we can begin to develop the compassionate, helpful spirit seen in the good Samaritan and so warmly commended by Jesus.

First, we need to cultivate the habit of looking at life's wounded ones through the eyes of Jesus. Though the legalists who dragged the adulterous woman into his presence wanted to stone her, Jesus looked through the eyes of a compassionate God and wanted to save her from her sins. He saw things which the would-be-stoners did not see: not only her potential when redeemed, but some experiences in her past which had tripped her and had made the way of righteousness hard for her wayward feet. Seen in this spirit, the woman deserved saving, not stoning.

Through the same compassionate eyes Jesus looked into the lives of other sinful, obstinate, wounded people and saw their past with understanding and sorrow. He saw their potential for future usefulness and joy, and touched them with a lifting, transforming power. Seeing in their hearts some hungers and frustrations which their condemning society did not see, and seeing in their abilities large usefulness for the future, he dealt with them as society never had.

He looked upon the sick, the lame, the blind, the leprous—and his heart was so moved with compassion that he often wept. He looked upon the lonely, the discouraged, and the sorrowing with an understanding heart. If we want to become good Samaritans, we shall need to make sure that we look at life's wounded people through the eyes of Jesus and not through the eyes of a society which is too quick to condemn.

Second, having achieved the capacity to look at people through the eyes of Jesus, we shall find it easier to react to the needs of these unfortunate people through the heart of Jesus. Our love, sympathy, patience, and long-suffering may wear thin; but if we pray and strive until we come to have a heart like his, there will be no limits to the distance to which our hearts will go in reaching out to "impossible" people. With a heart like his, we shall have a touch like his!

Third, we need to develop an unselfishness of motivation like that of Christ. His purpose for being on the earth was to do the will of God. The very meat which sustained him here, according to his own testimony, was doing the will of God. Therefore, his ministries to people who had made grave mistakes and in whose lives there were urgent needs were not tailored to the praise, publicity, appreciation, or material compensation which came. Because he so much loved his Father God, he rejoiced to do the things which brought joy to his father's heart. He knew that he would not be doing the will of God if he did not translate into his actions the love of God, and the consciousness of having pleased God meant infinitely more to him than the plaudits of men.

With eyes and heart and motivation patterned after the life of Jesus, we shall have in our lives some inevitable characteristics of Christlikeness which will distinguish our ministries to the robbed and wounded with a winsome attractiveness. Thoughtfulness, courtesy, sympathy, understanding, patience, optimism, happiness of spirit, and tender tactfulness are some of the fruits of the Christlike spirit in dealing with those whose lives have been touched with hurt. When these characteristics are woven into our lives, the very manner in which we minister will remind people of Jesus.

A college professor spent nearly fifty years in dedicated teaching and living on a small campus. Though he was never officially responsible for anything except his teaching, he literally took to his heart the needy students, the students who had difficulties with their studies, and the students who ran afoul of the college regulations. His heart and purse were constantly poured out in behalf of the students with financial needs. His time was given almost limitlessly to helping the slow and plodding students. Though he never condoned the wrongdoing of any student who came up for discipline, he felt himself Christ-bound to try valiantly to help every student who needed rehabilitation.

As this distinguished professor's body lay in state in the college chapel for a full day prior to the funeral, great hosts of admiring friends came and went. Their eulogies to his great heart were filled with reminiscences of his good Samaritan actions for nearly a half-century. Some paused to testify that they would have been on society's junk heap had this wonderful Christian not paused to "pour on the oil of sympathy and bind up their wounds with help." As his body was lowered into the grave, there was a silent, but universal feeling that he had left the richest legacy of Christlike ministry to students in need ever known in those parts.

The world has never had as many people in need of Christian ministry scattered along the roadside of everyday living as it has now. Though there may be an overplus of priests and Levites going on their selfish, hurried ways, there is not a surplus of followers of the good Samaritan in our day. The needs are urgent. The gratification from Christlike ministering is incomparably thrilling. Why not join up with the "Good Samaritan Corps" today?

7. Three Crosses

*And he bearing his cross went forth
into a place called the place of a skull,
which is called in the Hebrew Golgotha: where they crucified him, and
two other with him, on either side
one, and Jesus in the midst.*

JOHN 19:17–18

IN KEEPING WITH THE WIDESPREAD CUS-
tom of using significant terminology in lesser or lighter
ways than its meaning ever intended, many Christians
have fallen upon the habit of referring to almost any
difficulty as "a cross." It is needful, therefore, that all
Christians reappraise the experiences which have so
quickly and so thoughtlessly been classified as crosses
to see if they may be accurately so called.

On Golgotha that day there stood three crosses. Two
of them were man-made, for the men who occupied
them were drawing down upon themselves the penalty
which society of their day exacted for their sins against
it. Those two crosses were neither God-sent nor were
they results of the permissive will of God; therefore,
they can never be classified in the same realm with the

73

cross on which the sinless Son of God was dying. If they be called crosses at all, they must be classified as "man-made crosses." Only that third cross was a cross in the truest spiritual sense of the word: an experience which comes, not as a normal development of life, not by the failure and sin of the individual who suffers, but by the permissive will of God for a purpose greater than the cost of the suffering entailed.

The first misnomer to which so many Christians have become accustomed is that of calling some difficulty a cross, when that difficulty is no more than a normal development of life. Just as night is a normal part of the span of day, just as winter is a normal part of the pattern of the seasons, just as storms are a normal part of the variety of weather, just as tragedy is an integral part of the scheme of drama, some difficulties are a normal part of the pattern of life. Therefore, to call such experiences "crosses" is to indicate a feeling that life was meant to be bereft of all experiences except the pleasant ones.

The housewife has to contend with perpetual repairs to the house, or the car seems difficult to keep in repair, or there is a continuing servant problem: these are difficulties which surely vex, but they are no more than normal difficulties and are misnamed if alluded to as crosses. A man runs into difficulties in his business or profession, or finds some phase of his work particularly burdensome; or the student finds the going hard in his studies or in his adjustment of study to work: these, too, are normal experiences for the pattern of life and are not correctly classified as crosses.

So often these normal difficulties are magnified by the mind-set of the individual who regards them as crosses, or as experiences which were not meant to be. With that attitude, he is robbed of the resilience of spirit with which he could otherwise tackle his difficulties constructively. If, however, there is the acceptance of the difficulties as a normal balance and comple-. ment the many happy experiences of life, the individual is not greatly surprised at their coming and is surely more likely to solve such problems earlier, or to take them in stride splendidly if they have come to stay.

The second group of experiences which are incorrectly called "crosses" are those which we pull down upon ourselves through obstinacy, neglect, inefficiency, or wilful violation of established principles. It is in this classification that the so-called crosses of the thieves on Golgotha would appear. They had consciously violated society's laws concerning theft; they knew from the beginning what the penalty would be; they had, therefore, simply come into the logical result of their deliberate acts. Limitations, losses, sufferings, or handicaps which come to us through wilful violation of our better knowledge are, likewise, not genuine crosses: they are the inevitable results of our own failures.

A woman who married against her best judgment and against the counsel of all her friends came inevitably to the result she could have anticipated: her marriage broke up, and she was left with several children.

Her frequent allusion to the "great cross" which she was called upon to bear left her friends a little irritated, since she had so wilfully walked into this inevitable result. Another woman, whose completely possessive and dictatorial disposition drove her husband away, similarly complained of the cross she had to bear; but she, too, has mislabeled her experience.

The individual who disregards the rules of health, the advice of doctors and counselors, the instructions for progress or success and comes upon failure or permanent handicap does not have the right to call his unhappy state a cross either. Even though the result to the individual is a very great hardship, it is but a dividend of his neglect, obstinacy, inefficiency, or wilful living. Though this individual may well regret the circumstances which brought the unhappy result, he does not have the right to classify his suffering as a cross. Or, let us be reminded, if such experiences are called crosses, the prefix "man-made" should be applied.

The only experiences which may be called crosses in the high spiritual sense of the word are those experiences which come, not as a result of any failure on the part of the individual, but as a part of the *plan* or *permission* of the will of God for purposes which are so great that the immediate suffering which the individual is called upon to undergo will be seen eventually to be justified in light of the accomplishment of the great purposes. The suffering may be precipitated, as in the case of Jesus, by the sin and failure of society or of some individual; yet, the individual to whom the suffering comes is thereby given an opportunity to demonstrate the power of God to achieve victory over apparently insuperable odds or even over the evil designs of others. Such victory not only makes of the individual a glorius victor but also gives to others of his time, and subsequent times, an example which lifts and strengthens.

Into this category fall many of the most heroic experiences of people in all the centuries of Christianity. Among these cross-bearers have been numbered many whose sacrifices have advanced the cause of Christianity and have glorified the triumph of the Christian faith in numberless communities of our earth. Let us consider three kinds of cross-bearers in this heroic group.

I

There are those into whose lives come tragedies of personal nature, tragedies which they could not prevent, but which they accept and turn into magnificent victory. Physical infirmities of every kind, losses which would normally overwhelm, disappointments which would usually embitter have come to these people; yet, in the spirit of Philippians 4:13, "I can do all things through Christ which strengtheneth me," they have turned numberless tragedies into triumphs of Christian faith.

I stood at the side of a young woman who had been in an iron lung since she was fourteen years of age. She

was now twenty-two. She had become the very greatest inspiration to her church, to her community, and
to her county of 150,000 people. She had committed
to memory the content of the sixteen courses required
for graduation from the high schools of her area and
had been honored in a diploma-conferring ceremony
which was widely pictured by the press. She thought
up and directed clever banquet programs and decora-
tions for the activities of her church. She had become
so incisive in her understanding of many portions of
the Bible that groups met at her home almost every
week to hear her devotional talks.

Though I knew the secret of her victory, I asked her
about it. Her reply was thrilling! "When it occurred
to me that I would be in this iron lung for the rest
of my life," she said, "it also occurred to me that Jesus,
who turned a cruel cross into the world's most inspiring symbol of victory, could help me to turn this
iron lung into a symbol of victory of Christian faith.
That is the explanation."

A lovely woman of almost threescore and ten years
had impressed me as having a face almost completely
free of any lines of worry and tension. Furthermore,
she was constantly inquiring concerning the well-being
of others, going out of her way to offer optimism and
help. My natural surmise was that her life had been
free from the cares which so constantly bring lines of
great tension into the faces of others.

Can you imagine my surprise at learning later of the
state of affairs which had been hers? Her only child had

been born with almost incredible abnormalities and she had looked after him with loving care for forty years. Her husband had been paralyzed and speechless for over twelve years prior to his death, and she had looked after him with inspiring devotion. Her ninety-five-year old mother was bedridden and almost deaf, but this devoted daughter kept her in her own home for personal care and supervision. I have never seen a more radiant cross-bearer!

II

A second group of genuine cross-bearers is made up of those heroic men and women who have suffered for their efforts in behalf of the advancement of the well-being of mankind in many fields. Ridicule, malignant falsehoods, the cup of hemlock, the cruel rack, the burning stake, lonely exile, and myriad other inhumanities have been the rewards for their heroic efforts to advance the learning, to widen the horizons, and to lift the loads of their fellow men. In science, sociology, economics, exploration, health, justice, religion, and in the composite efforts of men to elevate the dignity of man, there have been so many illustrious cross-bearers.

Although these heroes are too numerous to number or mention, the reader will supply their names and will observe these two truths running through their experiences like golden cords: (1) these heroes who bore their crosses so well are now immortal in reputation, influence, and inspiration; (2) their works have so well lived after them that they have come to be regarded as magnificent contributors to society's progress. Some of the principles for which these people suffered and died are today so completely accepted by most of our world that we take them for granted and are astonished that anyone ever did refuse to accept them. Humanity stands in everlasting debt to these magnificent cross-bearers.

III

A third group of these genuine cross-bearers is comprised of those who have suffered heroically and victoriously for the advancement of the cause of Christ in our world. From the very beginning of Christianity the cross has been the "hallmark" of advancement. Jesus made this crystal clear in many of his utterances. Luke presents his unmistakably clear indication that people who wish to be "just like him" may expect the cross: "If anyone wants to follow in my footsteps, he must give up all right to himself, carry his cross every day and keep close behind me" (9:23, Phillips).

No truer explanation of genuine cross-bearing could be voiced than that in the words, "he must give up all right to himself, carry his cross every day. . . ." Crucifying self, taking whatever is the cost of following Jesus completely, though the cost may vary from individual to individual, is indeed genuine cross-bearing! Jesus gave up all right to himself long before he was nailed to Golgotha's cross, for in coming to the earth and in pouring out his life so limitlessly in the years of tension-filled ministry he was bearing a cross constantly.

From the earliest days of Christianity those who have borne the cause of Christ to its most significant advancement were called upon to give up all right to themselves and to pay so dearly. Stephen, Paul, Peter, and the other disciples not only suffered greatly: some of them were called upon to die because of their fidelity to the cause of Christ. After them have come other cross-bearers through the centuries. The cross, the stake, the gallows, the whipping post, the dungeon cells of prisons, the catacombs, and a thousand other symbols of their suffering have become points of inspiration in the history of Christianity. Even today in many parts of our world the followers of Christ are called upon to suffer. Our missionaries undertake unbelievable privations with delight, and heroic servants of our Lord deny the selfish demands of the flesh in order to facilitate the preaching of the gospel.

IV

Have you ever borne a cross for Christ? Have you ever even undertaken anything of great difficulty for Christ? Have you ever actually denied yourself anything of importance and value to you in order to advance his cause? Have you ever suffered anything for Christ? Have you accepted a privation, discomfort, inconvenience, or sacrifice for the cause of his church in the sense, "This is the least I can do, and I shall do it gladly"? Have you ever denied yourself an indulgence of some wish, even something which you have normally felt to be a necessity, because you felt that the money involved was so much more urgently needed for Christian missions?

Paul made inescapably clear in Romans 12:1-2 that you and I should be willing to make of our lives "living sacrifices," and he made the appeal even more binding by saying, in effect, that it is only a "reasonable service" on your part and mine. In short, it is reasonable that you and I be willing to bear crosses in our lives when we remember that the Son of God very literally died for us! It would surely be reasonable for us to go to any lengths to prove worthy of a fireman's death in our behalf. It is even more reasonable that the Christian make of his life a living sacrifice, that he become a surrendered, victorious cross-bearer.

There was a wonderful woman connected with a Christian college for many years. Through all the years of her connection she gave up all right to herself and immersed herself in the life of the college, regardless of the time and energy required. She gave no evidence ever of feeling underpaid, underpraised, or underpublicized. She did menial tasks during wartime when servants were hard to obtain. She gladly sacrificed the quantity and quality of clothes which she could have afforded, because there were students who needed help. She even denied herself the convenience of a car and gladly rode public conveyances in order to give more generously to church and mission causes. If someone, by chance, discovered the tremendous sacrifice which she was making and sought to praise her, she looked both surprised and disappointed!

At the time of her death, great numbers of people, who had been bound to secrecy during her lifetime, came forward to attest the almost incredible lengths of self-effacement and self-denial to which she had gone during her years of Christian service. Many of her closest friends, though conscious of her complete unselfishness, were amazed and shamed by the magnificent spirit in which she had borne a cross of self-denial. One friend recalled receiving this reply to an attempt to praise her: "Our Lord did not ask for an easy time when our well-being was involved, and I feel that I do not have the right to ask for more than the opportunity to be like him."

The only Christians who arrive at the fullest degree of fellowship with Jesus are the cross-bearers. There is a degree of fellowship, peace, joy, and thrill in meeting Jesus from underneath our crosses which can come in no other way. Only then do we come to realize the joyous truth that his yoke is easy and his burden is light.

8. Three Calls for Tears

Jesus wept. JOHN 11:35

W E RECALL THAT LAZARUS, DEVOTED and beloved friend of Jesus, fell seriously ill. Though Jesus was advised of the illness, he did not arrive in Bethany until Lazarus had died and was buried. After a tearful greeting from Martha and Mary, Jesus and the mourners proceeded to the grave in which Lazarus had been buried. It was as Jesus beheld the group's weeping that he, too, wept.

We can understand immediately why a mere man would have wept at a time like that. In the light of man's limitation of understanding and power, and in the light of his sense of personal loss in the going of a friend, tears would have been so normal for an earthbound man. Yet, Jesus suffered no limitation of knowledge and power and evidently had the intention to raise Lazarus from death. The factors which normally bring tears to you and me were evidently not at play in this instance.

Though the marvelously compassionate heart of Je-

sus and his tender feeling for any who suffer could be
an adequate explanation of those tears, there may well
have been other reasons for his tears. What may have
been some of the other factors which called forth these
tears of Jesus? The reader will understand that the
author is not saying that the three reasons to be discussed here *were* the factors which called forth the
tears; rather, he is saying that these three factors are
of such significance that they could have evoked the
tears of Jesus.

I

Jesus may well have wept at the failure of Martha
and Mary to understand the promises of Christianity
to its followers concerning sorrow, suffering, disappointment, difficulty, and death.

Both Martha and Mary had said to him, "Lord, if
thou hadst been here, our brother had not died" (John
11:21,32). If they meant to be saying that Jesus had
the power to keep Lazarus from dying, they were
gloriously correct. If, however, they meant to imply
that, had Jesus arrived earlier, he would not have
permitted Lazarus to die, they were absolutely wrong.
The fact that they and Lazarus had been deeply devoted to Christ was no justification for expecting to
be exempt from life's hardships and losses.

Christ never promised his followers *exemption* from
the hard experiences of life. In fact, both his example
and his invitation to discipleship offer just the opposite
of exemption. Jesus himself was a man of sorrows and

acquainted with grief. From his birth in a rude stable, through years of labor in Nazareth, through tension-packed years of harassment in his public ministry, through Gethsemane, and through Golgotha he moved —always facing difficulties and disappointments. His example surely offers no basis for the presumption that his followers may expect to find the following of Jesus to be an easy way.

Christ's invitation to discipleship is, likewise, no basis for the expectation that his followers will be exempt from cross-bearing. That invitation is given clearly as Jesus calls each follower to carry his cross every day. Carrying one's cross every day surely implies that the Christian will face times of great difficulty and even times of travail.

Though Christ did not promise exemption from the sorrows and sufferings of life, and though he did not promise that we would not face death, he did promise to give us victory over both life and death. Paul, who had experienced victory in a life beset with myriad difficulties, cried out in joy, "I can do all things through Christ which strengtheneth me" (Phil. 4:13). As he looked forward to the demands of the future, he asserted with joyous confidence, "But my God shall supply all your need according to his riches in glory by Christ Jesus" (Phil. 4:19).

These glorious assurances mean that, though the Christian will not be exempt from bearing loads, God's power will always be adequate; though he will not be exempt from temptation, with every temptation there will be provided a way of escape; though he will not be excused from sorrow, with his sorrow there will be songs in the night and bright stars of hope in his firmament of darkness; though he will not be spared disappointments, God's wisdom and power and love will turn these disappointments into milestones of progress toward victory; though he will not be exempt from death, he will find that the sting has been removed from death, and that victory has been taken from the grave.

What more can the reasonable Christian ask? How inconsistent it is, therefore, for us to fret and complain at life's vicissitudes, as if their coming were unfair or unnatural in the life of a Christian! If toil, travail, heartache, and crucifixion came to the sinless Son of God, it becomes almost ridiculous for the highly imperfect ones of us who are his followers to expect to be exempt simply because we are his devoted followers. It is not surprising that the tears of Jesus were called forth if Martha and Mary meant to be implying that Jesus would have excused them from this experience because of their devotion to him.

II

Another factor which could have evoked these tears of Jesus was Martha's evident lack of faith in the power of Jesus to accomplish here and now a triumph which imperfect faith had not thought possible. The basis of this observation is found in Martha's response to Jesus' resurrection suggestion:

But I know, that even now, whatsoever thou wilt
ask of God, God will give it thee. Jesus saith
unto her, Thy brother shall rise again. Martha
saith unto him, I know that he shall rise again
in the resurrection *at the last day*. Jesus
saith unto her, *I am the resurrection,* and the
life: he that believeth in me, though he were
dead, yet shall he live (John 11:22–25, italics added) .

It seemed not to dawn upon Martha that the Lord of
the resurrection could accomplish resurrection then
and there without waiting for "the last day" to which
she had referred. Though she believed that he was the
Christ, the Son of God, and that whatever he should
ask of God would be given, her faith evidently did not
extend to such limits as to believe that Jesus could
overcome time and circumstances to the extent of
making resurrection possible immediately. Despite her
profession of faith in his power, she was still thinking
in finite terms. Even when Jesus suggested that the
stone be removed from Lazarus' grave, Martha's faith
seemed not to have caught up the intent and impact
of the power of her Christ, for she questioned the re-
moval of the stone.

Jesus, pinpointing the thrilling potential of a limitless faith, said to Martha and to all of us, "Did I not
tell you that if you would believe you would see the
glory of God?" (John 11:40, RSV) . The very logical
converse of that statement is that we miss seeing the
glory of God demonstrated in our lives and in circumstances with which we have to do because *we do not*

believe to the limits to which faith wants to take us.

Jesus may well be weeping today, as he wept that day, at the lack of a vital, immediate, adequate faith in the lives of so many of his followers. Though we know that we belong to an omnipotent God, we are prone to make plans as if only our own limited resources were available to accomplish those plans. We literally creep along, borne down often to the crushing point by problems and burdens, and do not call upon God for power and wisdom; or we do not call upon him until we have been practically crushed. Instead of permitting God to be an ever-present help, our limited faith consigns him to an emergency status, to be called upon only in dire extremities.

If you and I should really believe the promises of God's Word to the followers of Christ and to his church, and if we should really apply that faith to our lives and to the program of his church, the world would be amazed by the results. We have cheated ourselves, his church, and our world of victory and power because we, too, apply so poorly the faith which our lips have confessed that our hearts believe. As Jesus contemplates this lack of applied faith in our lives today, he may so well be weeping again!

III

The third factor which may well have called forth the tears of Jesus was the behavior of these two followers of his in the face of the death of an excellent Christian. The Jews who accompanied the procession to

Lazarus' grave were weeping: it was logical that they weep, for they were evidently nonbelieving Jews and, therefore, did not believe in the resurrection. But Martha and Mary were weeping, too; and, at least by implication, there was no difference in their weeping from the weeping of those who neither believed in Jesus nor in his promise of the resurrection.

Though the recourse to tears on the part of Martha and Mary was a normal reaction and, therefore, not to be condemned, there should have been a testimony, even through their tears, that they were *not* weeping for the same reasons for which the nonbelievers wept. They had a blessed hope not possessed by their Jewish friends; therefore, the disconsolate note of the nonbelievers' weeping was not in place in the tears of Christians who mourned the loss, for a time only, of a beloved Christian.

Though tears are as normal as heartaches at times in which death takes loved ones from our sight for a while, the Christian ought to demonstrate his faith in victory over death, even through his tears. Though weeping, the Christian's witness at the bier of a loved one who died in Christ should be saying to all about: "I am weeping for my temporary loss, and not that I feel that a tragedy has befallen this loved one who has gone to be with Jesus. The most wonderful release and promotion imaginable have come to this loved one. It would be inconsistent to wish to rob him of the magnificence of being with the Lord. I weep, therefore, not for him, but for myself; for I shall be lonely in the days ahead."

In the funeral services of a college student who had died of a malady which had limited his strength for years, that student's physics professor delivered the message. In simple eloquence he pointed out the wonderful promotion which had come to the departed student: whereas his strength had been limited for years, he was now clothed in the power of an omnipotent God and would never again feel a sense of frustration; whereas, despite his very bright mind, he had been hampered by the finiteness of all earth's minds, he was now able to see the universe through the omniscient mind of the God who had made it; whereas he was a good musician here on our earth, he had been promoted to heaven's orchestras and would never again be limited in the scope of his understanding and performance of exquisite music.

In concluding his quiet but meaningful message, the professor pointed out that the proper attitude for the Christian was not to wish the departed student back among us to be limited as before, but to feel a sense of joy and congratulation at his release and promotion. Jesus surely did not weep as he beheld that funeral, for even the departed student's family reflected the glorious conviction of triumph which the speaker had voiced.

IV

Jesus loves you and me just as personally and as tenderly as he loved Martha, Mary, and Lazarus. His loving, sensitive heart reacts with joy or with sorrow to what he sees when he looks into our lives today. Does he see childish expectations and reactions to life's normal developments? Does he see tragic losses in our lives because we do not believe with great faith? Does he see that we do not behave as victorious Christians should behave in the face of death? Does he see intolerance, intemperance, indifference, disobedience, and sin—twisting, marring, and maiming our lives and hurting Christianity's witness to our world?

Let us imagine that a scribe is writing, recording the reaction of Jesus as he looks into your life or mine today. Let's peep over the shoulder of the scribe to see what he is writing. In speaking of the reaction of Jesus, the scribe has already written, "As he looked into the life of ————." Will the next words be "Jesus wept" or "Jesus smiled"?

PART THREE

Are You Living Consistently?

Are You Driving with Your Brake On?

Can You Afford That Emotion?

Are You Afraid to Die?

In Which
The Christian Is Bidden to Ask
Himself Four Frank Personal
Questions. In Answering These
Questions Honestly the Christian
Will Discover Still Other Areas
in Which He Needs to Dare to
Apply the Teachings of Christi-
anity Consistently and Coura-
geously.

9. Are You Living Consistently?

For if the trumpet give an uncertain
sound, who shall prepare himself to
the battle?   1 CORINTHIANS 14:8

IN MANY INSTANCES IN GOD'S WORD
we find the rhetorical question used—a question asked,
not to evoke an answer from the lips of the reader or
hearer, but to provoke thought and subsequent answer in the heart of the reader or listener. Such a
question is asked in 1 Corinthians 14:8.

From the suggestion of that verse a military situation comes into our minds. On the one hand are the
commanding officers who know exactly the best action
for the armed forces to take next. On the other hand
are tens of thousands of men in battle gear, aware that
a battle is imminent, waiting with doubly keen ears for
the call of the trumpet to indicate the next action. Between the commanding officers and the armed forces
stand the trumpeters, who, in the days in which this
verse was given to us, were the only means of com-

munication between officers and the men who waited for orders.

The hopes of the commanders depended upon an accurate relay of their orders to the men who waited to do battle. The confidence and lives of the men who waited to follow the commanders' orders depended upon clear and unmistakable orders relayed by the trumpeters. The trumpeters, therefore, could frustrate the hopes of the commanders and send the soldiers into confusion and despair by sounding an "uncertain sound," leaving the men with uncertainty and confusion concerning what they should do next. In some instances, life and victory depended upon whether or not the trumpeters gave clear, clarion, unmistakable directions through their trumpet calls.

Now, from this military figure, what lesson can be drawn for our everyday Christian living? To this writer, the following seems to be a fair analogy: on one hand stands Christ, wanting so earnestly to "get through" to people who do not know him; on the other hand stand those people who do not know Christ; between Christ and those people stand Christians like you and me, who say that we know and follow Christ and who are, therefore, logically regarded as examples of the Christ-controlled life.

Christ depends as significantly upon Christians to get his compassionate love and transforming power through to unsaved people as the military commanders depended upon the trumpeters long ago. Unsaved people, many of who do not attend church and do not read Bibles, have as their only opportunity of seeing Christ the daily living of Christians around them. If the daily lives of these Christians are a flesh-and-blood translation of the spirit and teachings of Jesus, their lives become clear and attractive "trumpet calls," inviting unsaved people to follow Jesus.

But what if the lips of the Christian say one thing, and his life lives an entirely different thing? What if he professes one thing and practices another? What if his Sunday life and his weekday life are contradictory? Such a life is giving an "uncertain sound," and non-Christians will be confused. They will say, in effect, "Shall we follow what your lips say or what your life lives? Shall we obey your professing or shall we pattern after your practicing? Shall we imitate your Sunday life or your weekday life?" The tragic result of this confusion in the minds of many unsaved persons is that they will turn away with disappointment, disillusionment, and even bitterness. Some may never follow Jesus because of inconsistent Christians.

What kind of trumpet call does your life give? Is it a confusing, disappointing sound of contradiction; or is it a clear, consistent, attractive challenge to follow Jesus? Perhaps it will be helpful to all of us to examine the consistency with which we are living our Christianity in several areas of life common to most of us.

I

We need to live our Christianity consistently *at home*. The touchstone of the genuineness of your

Christianity and mine is how we live it within the four walls of home. If we are living the spirit and teachings of Christ in the family circle, our public impact for Christianity will carry warmth and power. If we are not living Christianity at home, there will be a hollow ring to our public preachments, and the sensitive hearts of searching people will discern that something is wrong. Suppose that people have been impressed of our apparent sweetness and fineness as we appeared or performed in church on Sunday; then suppose they could peep in on us when we are at our normal behavior at home. Would those people think more highly or less highly of our Christianity?

Husbands, what do your wives think of your Christianity? Do their hearts respond warmly to your public prayers and public utterances concerning Christianity, because they know that in the day-by-day relationships at home you are just as sincere and fervent? Wives, as you sing beautifully in chorus or solo, or as you present some thoughts before a church group, do your husbands' hearts rejoice in the knowledge that you are even more wonderful in your warm Christian testimony at home? Parents, what do your children think of the genuineness of your Christianity in the light of home conversations, attitudes, ideals, and behavior? Children, do your parents rejoice at any compliments given upon your public performances in religious activities because they have the happy knowledge that you are radiantly consistent in your Christian living at home?

I had suggested at the conclusion of a message on sin that every member of that night's congregation complete the service in a time of confession before retiring. The wife of a man who had already impressed me as having a wonderfully radiant countenance said to me on the following day, "I honestly wondered what he could confess, for he is the finest person I have ever met." A husband said of his wife, "I have lived with her for twenty-five years and I have never known her to be little or mean in spirit." Two boys, speaking of their father, said to me, "He is the finest man we ever knew: you just couldn't grow up around him without *wanting* to do right." Two parents said of their only child, "We have learned more about Christianity from the way in which she lives it at home than we had ever known before."

A university student was untouched by my appeal that he not commit a dangerous act because, I had stressed the fact, his mother would be disappointed. It turned out, to my dismay, that his mother's church life and home life were as different as night and day! Another lad, who had developed a strong antipathy for church life, was a son of parents who were outstanding lay leaders in the church and who, to all appearances, were paragons of good parenthood. To the counselor closest to him, the boy eventually confided that his parents drank alcoholic beverages privately at home, were often contemptuous of other people in the church, and were anything but Christians when on vacation! The mother of a high school beauty queen confided in me that the daughter led two lives: a smiling, gracious, charming life in public, but a selfish, demanding, haughty life at home.

Every one of us needs to ask himself this question: *Do I constantly, consistently live my Christianity at home?*

II

Christians need to live Christianity *at work*. If Christians throughout our nation, working in daily contact with other employees, should live the Christian teachings and portray the Christlike spirit through one work week, the impact would be tremendous. The increase in church attendance and in conversions would be phenomenal, for fellow workers would be searching for the source of power which had made their work-time associates so winsome and likable.

If the employees with whom you work were asked to name the best Christians they know, would your name be on some lists . . . many lists? They are the ones who saw and heard you when you bumped your shin on that chair or when you set the typewriter down on a finger. They know your attitudes toward your work and whether or not you give an honest day's work for the compensation received. They know whether or not you are Christian in your attitudes toward employers and fellow employees. They noticed that you did or did not participate in the acrid criticism of some absent employee. They have seen you when you were tired and upset or when you were unjustly accused. They have not heard you make talks about Christianity, but they have seen and heard your life.

A supervisor told me of an employee whose quiet, Christian spirit moved steadily through an entire floor of workers. There was no opportunity for speech-making on her part: just the day-by-day living of the spirit and teachings of Jesus. A shop manager, who dedicated his life to a closer walk with Jesus, so shared with twenty employees his new spirit and joy that the atmosphere of that repair shop was transformed. A dentist's helper told me that on many days she left her work with the feeling that she had been in church all day because her employer diffused so much Christian spirit throughout the duties of the day. A Negro porter in a huge metropolitan railway station has permeated his work with Christian philosophy so thoroughly through the years that he is a much respected and sought after employee of that vast institution.

If you should truly, consistently live the spirit and teachings of Christ for one full week in the place or institution in which you work, would your fellow workers be impressed of remarkable differences in you? If so, you have evidently not been as completely Christian in your working hours in the days agone, and there ought to be some changes made!

III

Christian students need to live Christianity *at school*. If the students of the school which you attend, student reader, were asked to list the three best Christians of their acquaintance in that school, on how many lists would your name appear? These students would not be listing you because of speeches you have made, regardless of their eloquence. They would be listing you on the basis of the way in which you have lived your Christianity in the classrooms, in the science laboratories, in the cafeteria lines, in the library, in the dormitory, on the hallways, on the playing fields, in the rehearsal times, and in the diverse activities of leisure hours. Have they been witnessing the clear demonstration of Christianity in your character, conduct, and spirit? Can they point to definite instances in which you have been truly Christian, despite the difficulties involved?

I visited in a large senior high school in which the assembly conduct was as worshipful as if we had sat in the sanctuary of a church. When I shared with the principal my feeling that the spirit of the school was unusually fine, he told me the reason. A football star, feeling that the spirit of the squad was not wholesome, suggested to the coach that every practice time and every game be begun with a squad prayer time. Not only did the performance and spirit of the team undergo transformation but the daily living of the football men began to show such differences that the entire student body "caught the glow." On each school morning, prior to the first bell, in the largest classroom in the school building, approximately 150 students assembled for prayer. The entire school had experienced a change of spirit because one student put his Christianity into action.

In several fraternities which I have visited on college and university campuses, the amazingly fine spirit of those groups was explained in terms of one student who insisted upon living his Christian principles so consistently and attractively that the entire group was permeated by a happy, Christian spirit. Some professional clubs on campuses had begun to veer toward the ribald in social functions but have been brought back to Christian good taste by the consistent, attractive Christian courage of one or two members. One high school group whose annual social big time had become almost an alcoholic beverage binge was steered back to sanity and stability by the courageous testimony of a student officer who dared to be a Christian witness.

In one of the senior high schools of my city there was an outstanding Christian student in the editorship of the school paper. In returning from a nearby town with the proofs of the paper one Monday morning he lost his life in a car accident. From his shirt pocket two items were taken. One was a New Testament, well read and marked. The other item was a note card. On one side of the card he had written his chores for the day; on the other side he had written these graphic words: "You must be very careful of the life you lead; you are the only Bible some people will read." He had remembered so wonderfully what every Christian student needs to remember: the consistent daily living of

Christian spirit and teachings in school relationships may provide the only opportunity which some unsaved students have to come to know what Christianity really is.

IV

Christians throughout our nation, regardless of age, need so urgently to be reminded of the importance of living their Christianity in social and recreational activities. A man just converted from a life of much dissipation said, "If just the people of America who are called Christians would stop drinking alcoholic beverages, the distilleries would probably find their operations unprofitable; and if the church members who now go to race tracks to gamble would not go, the profits of those operations would show a terrific decline." He put his finger accurately, even if painfully, upon one of the greatest needs of Christianity in America today: the need for Christians to be positively Christian in their social and recreational activities!

In our leisure-time associations, as in the associations discussed in earlier paragraphs, we are constantly in touch with people who need a tug toward Christ. In the happiness and relaxation of the right kind of social and recreational activity, living our Christianity joyously and winsomely, we have unparalleled opportunities to draw people toward Christ. On the other hand, our participation in questionable social and recreational activities, or our participation in wholesome activities in a spirit of thoughtlessness or discourtesy toward others or in a letdown of Christian principle in conversation or activity can so easily invalidate a lifetime of apparently sincere speechmaking in behalf of Christianity. We need to be such radiant, winsome Christians in our social and recreational lives that unsaved people who have played with us will respond with warm interest to the invitation to pray with us!

A student once told me that he did not wish to hear any more religious talks delivered by a rather eloquent student speaker on his campus. His reason? He and the student speaker had double-dated on the preceding Saturday night; he had been greatly disappointed in the compromising behavior of his erstwhile Christian ideal. Similarly, a beautiful and talented young woman could not be used in keeping with her excellent abilities in the youth program of her church because other young people knew of distressing lapses of behavior in her dating life. In both of these instances the behavior of Christians had given uncertain, discordant, disillusioning sounds to other young people, and had made them handicaps to Christianity.

A lay leader in a local church was eloquent in speech and versatile in ability. People who played golf with him, however, lost enthusiasm for his religious talks because of his poor sportsmanship on the golf course. They reported that he was dishonest in some of his procedures, ugly in spirit toward winners, unwilling to admit his own lack of excellence. One of his golf partners somewhat humorously said that this lay leader did not curse when he made a bad play, but that he spat vigorously; and that where he spat, no grass grew back!

But to close with a happier suggestion: this writer has personal knowledge of many wonderful instances in which unsaved people were drawn to church and then to Christ through the magnificent Christian spirit of people who had been winsomely, consistently Christian in their social and recreational relationships. In their playtime activities these Christians had given a clear, clarion, consistent "trumpet call."

On one campus there was a football star who won seven of his teammates to Christ, largely through his wholesomeness and joy in leisure hour activities. His buddies knew that he had something which they had missed! There is a swimming star who found that the younger boys who thronged to observe his heralded skill were asking, "What church do you attend?" A friend told me of a young woman whose date sensed such a difference in her from other girls whom he had dated that he concluded, "It must be your religion that makes you so wonderful!" Throughout America many Christians are finding that the application of Christianity to their social lives does not reduce their popularity or the number of friends they have; rather, it affords a thrilling and amazing opportunity for drawing other people to Christ.

At home, at work, at school, at play—what kind of trumpet call does *your* life give?

10. Are You Driving with Your Brake On?

> *Wherefore seeing we also are com-*
> *passed about with so great a cloud of*
> *witnesses, let us lay aside every weight,*
> *and the sin which doth so easily beset*
> *us, and let us run with patience the*
> *race that is set before us.*
>
> HEBREWS 12:1

Do YOU OCCASIONALLY PUT YOUR CAR into operation without releasing the hand brake? If so, you have joined the rest of us in discovering that the unreleased brake is all handicap. The unreleased brake brings greater wear and tear, larger consumption of oil and gas, and lessened efficiency of operation. In short, the unreleased brake is all dead weight and a positive impediment to progress.

There are Christians almost numberless throughout our world who are driving with their brakes on in spiritual living, too. They go through all the motions of being good Christians: they read their Bibles regularly, they pray faithfully, they attend church and participate in its activities fully, they give proportionately of their income; yet, they do not have peace of heart, joy of soul, continuing progress, and the thrilling victories which so many other Christians have. The simple answer to the question "Why" is that they are driving with some brakes unreleased!

These factors, like the weights mentioned in Hebrews 12:1, need to be laid aside so that the Christian may run the race with the maximum chance of victory. Though anything which slows down the Christian's spiritual growth, which robs him of confidence, which prohibits peace and joy is a weight which needs to be discarded, here is a list of ten common deterrents to spiritual victory which so many Christians need to lay aside.

I

Fear has robbed more Christians of happiness and victory than we can number. I do not refer to the wholesome fears given to us by God to safeguard us from danger and from foolish action. I refer to the unwholesome fears which God never intended that we entertain, fears which rob us of faith-based confidence as we go forward into the future, which deter us from attempting what God meant us to attempt, which keep us from witnessing and serving in keeping with our abilities and opportunities. These fears rob us of our rightful heritage of joy and victory as children of God through Jesus Christ.

Whence come these fears which cause us to worry

unduly about ourselves or our families or our friends, which put dark clouds of apprehension about today and tomorrow, and which sometimes paralyze us with terror and inaction? Their origin is no mystery; for, indeed, these fears are planted within us and tilled assiduously by the same Evil One who has sought from the Garden of Eden forward to frustrate the happiness and victory which God wants his children to have. Knowing that he cannot rob us of the salvation which our belief on Christ has brought, Satan devotes his energies to trying to blight our lives in a variety of ways, knowing that if he makes us unhappy Christians, we shall not be assets to God's plan or to Christianity. Fear is one of his most potent weapons in the perpetual attempt to invalidate Christian happiness and usefulness.

A splendid young man with an excellent voice told me that the very thought of standing before an audience to sing solos so terrified him that he was almost paralyzed with fear; therefore, he did not accept more than a few of the many opportunities to sing which came to him. He loved to sing; he wanted to sing; yet, this inordinate fear frustrated him. Feeling that the fear was not logical, he told me about it and asked my counsel.

I asked him if he had ever read 2 Timothy 1:7. He replied that, though he had read the Bible through, he could not immediately recall the verse. I passed my New Testament to him, so that he might have the joy of discovering the wonderful revelation which that verse brought. His eyes grew large with wonder and delight as he read: "For God hath not given us the spirit of fear; but of power, and of love, and of a sound mind."

Thereafter, I had no difficulty in pointing out two things to him: (1) that the God who had given to him the voice with which to sing could not consistently give the fear which kept him from singing; (2) that the probable source of the fear was the same person who, since Eden, has tried to keep God's children from becoming what God intended. That verse has become the key verse of that young man's life and has virtually eliminated the fears which had earlier beset him.

So many Christians do not win unsaved friends because fears have kept them from trying. Other Christians do not perform service in their churches which would bring joy to them and inspiration to others because Satan has implanted fears that they might not succeed, or that they might not perform as well as someone else could, or that someone might criticize or ridicule. What victories over the Christian are thus accomplished by Satan through his subtle weapon of fear!

When we remember that God's Word is so liberally filled with promises and assurances of God's presence and help, it becomes all the more tragic that Christians should be hampered by fear. Just to quote from one of the great galaxies of Bible assurances:

Fear thou not; for I am with thee: be not dismayed; for I am thy God: I will strengthen thee; yea, I

> will help thee; yea, I will uphold thee with the
> right hand of my righteousness. . . . For I the Lord
> thy God will hold thy right hand, saying unto thee,
> Fear not; I will help thee (Isa. 41:10,13).

A few other verses from the rich treasure of verses of assurance from God's Word are these: Deuteronomy 31:8, Joshua 1:9, Psalm 27:1, Mark 10:27, and Philippians 4:13 and 19.

When I was rushed from a roadside to a hospital, following a serious automobile accident in 1947, I realized that my already-lame left leg was so badly injured that amputation might be the only safe thing for the surgeons to do. While not confiding my fear to anyone, I found that the fear of losing that limb with subsequent added impairment to my walking—and, perhaps to my usefulness—grew and grew until the fear almost benumbed me. In the midst of those days there came to me a telegram from a group of nursing students. They gave their own expression of good wishes and listed a Bible reference, Isaiah 40:31.

Immediately I reached for my Bible to read the passage. You can understand what happened to the baseless fear in my heart when I read these marvelous words: "But they that wait upon the Lord shall renew their strength; they shall mount up with wings as eagles; they shall run, and not be weary; and they shall walk, and not faint." My fears subsided and departed in the light of this wonderful promise that, regardless of the outcome of my accident, all would be well with me. I would never have had the fear so long had I besought the Holy Spirit to lead me to passages of assurance. Somewhere in God's Word there is a passage, sometimes many passages, perfectly designed to relieve the Christian of any fear which ever comes!

II

Fears not laid aside grow into *anxiety,* which is an advanced state of fear. To be descriptive, let us say that fear is an ulcer and that anxiety is a malignancy. Anxiety will do for the Christian's psychological and spiritual well-being exactly what a malignancy will do for his physical body: it will debilitate and eventually kill his peace of mind, his joy of heart, his confidence in victory, his usefulness, and his influence. So, in laying aside fear, the Christian automatically saves himself from the development of anxiety. One of the most challenging and comforting verses in God's Word is "Throw the whole of your anxiety upon Him, because He cares for you" (1 Peter 5:7, Weymouth).

III

Doubt in the Christian's heart is another regular weapon from Satan's versatile arsenal. Knowing that the Christian is safe in the hands of God and that, according to the declaration of Jesus, no man can pluck him out of the Father's hand (John 10:29), Satan does not waste his time in trying the impossible. Instead, he concentrates on trying to wreck the confidence and usefulness of the Christian, thereby making his life of no account to Christ. If Satan can persuade the Chris-

tian to doubt that he has been saved, or to doubt that
Christ is the divine Son of God, or to doubt that Christ
was of virgin birth or that his bodily resurrection occurred, or to doubt that the Bible is the inspired Word
of God, he knows that he has won a tremendous victory.
The doubting Christian will not be a witnessing, serving, growing Christian and will not, therefore, attract
other people to Jesus.

What is the cure for doubt? We see this cure several
times in the earthly ministry of Christ. John the Baptist, in prison and scheduled for execution, was as-
sailed by the Tempter with the doubt that Jesus was
the promised Messiah. John did the smart thing: he
sent his doubts straight to Jesus by his disciples (Matt.
11:2–5), and those doubts disappeared because of what
those disciples saw and heard while with Jesus.
Thomas doubted that Christ could rise from the grave
and expressed his doubt emphatically in John 20:24–
29. In the presence of the Risen Christ a short time
later, however, his doubts were completely dispelled.
Throughout the earthly ministry of Jesus similar instances of doubt were dispelled when the doubters
made honest, openhearted contacts with him.

The cure today is the same. If now or later some
reader of these pages should be harassed by doubts
which disturb his faith and impede his spiritual progress, let him remember to bring those doubts to Christ.
He can do this through a rereading of our Lord's
earthly ministry, through fervent prayer, and through
sharing the doubts with trusted Christian friends and

counselors. Those doubts, too, will disappear in the bright light of the presence of Christ!

IV

Doubts not laid aside will grow into *disbelief*. The Christian who continues to doubt that he has been saved will come inevitably to disbelieve that he has experienced salvation. The Christian who doubts the deity of Christ, or his virgin birth, or his bodily resurrection long enough will come finally to disbelieve those great tenets of the Christian faith. The Christian who entertains doubts concerning the inspiration of the Scriptures sufficiently long will come to disbelieve that they are inspired. So, in laying aside doubt, the Christian prevents the later and heavier handicap of disbelief.

V

Sin is described in Hebrews 12:1 as a factor "which doth so easily beset us." Evidently, it should be laid aside. Sin has been variously described according to its impact of hurt in the Christian's life. Two of the most graphic descriptions of sin are these: (1) sin is a power leak through which much of the power which constructive habits bring into the life is lost; (2) sin is a disease spot, sending a steady stream of poisoning, paralyzing effect into the Christian's life.

The latter description is, perhaps, more in point in this discussion. For instance, in the physical body diseased tonsils can so affect physical fitness that eyesight, hearing, and general physical strength can be impaired. Diseased teeth can send enough poison into the system to bring a variety of physical infirmities. The only wise procedure is to "lay aside" these diseased tonsils or hopelessly diseased teeth. The analogy indicates that every habitual practice of sin is also a disease spot, and that the only hope of the Christian for full spiritual fitness is in his laying aside every habit of sinful nature. Otherwise, each sinful habit deters his growth and progress.

VI

Another deterring factor which needs to be laid aside is *self-satisfaction*—the being content with one's self, regardless of the probability that one's spiritual condition is far below the expectations of Christ. That kind of satisfaction breeds complacency and smugness with the result that not only does the Christian not grow, but he also becomes rather cynically proud of his present status. This condition leads inevitably to stagnation of spiritual growth, and stagnation leads inevitably to deterioration. Therefore, the self-satisfied Christian is not only not holding his own, but he is actually deteriorating.

The best and quickest cure for self-satisfaction comes through the individual's studying himself carefully in the light of the teachings of Jesus, putting himself under the microscope of the searching personal challenges for living, witnessing, and serving given in those teachings. Or, to put it differently, the Christian needs to stand up alongside Jesus for an accurate measurement of his life, to lay his life down alongside the teachings of Jesus to see how urgently he needs to improve. These measurements will bring a startling disclosure to the self-satisfied Christian, and the likelihood of his laying aside his contentment with self is very great.

VII

Another item of excess baggage which the Christian will need to lay aside is *false pride*. The pride which keeps us from admitting our weaknesses and our mistakes, which keeps us from apologizing and asking for pardon, which keeps us from confessing our sins to God in a spirit of utter truth and frankness, which keeps us from having the proper relationship of humility toward both God and man: these constitute false pride, a weapon of the Tempter, intended to be used effectively to rob us of spiritual power and progress.

When we contemplate the humility and love of our Saviour in giving up a throne of glory to come to a manger in a Bethlehem stable, his willingness to relinquish the fellowship of heaven for the monotony of Nazareth and the continuing conflict of ungrateful men around him, his willingness to exchange the exaltation of heaven's hosts for the humiliation on Golgotha, we no longer need to search for a pattern for our behavior in dealing with false pride.

Whatever we "give up" for Christian harmony, whatever pride we "swallow" in order to be Christlike will be so little in contrast to Christ's wonderful example. Until false pride goes out of our lives, the presence and winsomeness of Christ will never be seen in us; and we shall miss some of the finest victories of the Christian life!

VIII

Laziness robs an incalculably large number of Christians of continuing progress and gratifying victory. These Christians know the ways to victory in living, serving, and witnessing, but are unwilling to exercise the energies required to proceed down those ways.

Many Christians do not have the quality of prayer and devotional lives which they know to be essential to victorious living, because they are not willing to arise a bit earlier in the morning, or they are not willing to stay up a bit later at night to make possible an adequate time of Bible study and prayer. Though they know that there can be no great spiritual power without a powerful devotional life, they rationalize that they don't really have time, or that they just don't feel like doing anything that significant so early or so late, or that devotional habits of consequence are intended only for the leaders!

There are other Christians who are not serving in their churches in keeping with their capacities, because they do not want to have to make needed preparation, or attend necessary meetings, or be obligated to steady attendance and performance. Though they would never admit that the reason for their declining these normal activities of Christian growth is simple laziness, and though their lips may give rather beautiful words of explanation, the unattractive truth is that they are too lazy to prepare, to tackle, and to perform the duties for which they have the abilities.

Though this laziness may have physical aspects, it is primarily a spiritual laziness. If the spiritual awareness and ambition of the Christian are sufficiently strong, he *will* overcome any difficulty that threatens to impair his chance of spiritual growth and progress. Despite the fact that his physical body almost rebelled when the clock rang at 5:30 each morning, a student in one of our service academies had such a powerful urge to become strong in his spiritual powers that for four years in the academy he arose to read his Bible and to pray prior to the 6:15 rising hour of his fellow students. Laziness, despite its comfortable name, is a serious deterrent to victorious Christian living!

IX

Procrastination is not only a thief of time, according to the age-old proverb, but it is also a tremendous handicap to victorious Christian living. A sinister voice often seems to whisper to the Christian: "Yes, what you are thinking *is* the right thing to do, but there isn't any reason for doing anything about it right now . . . one of these days." And with that lulling reminder of intention to do the right thing some happy, easy day in the future, many Christians lose some of life's most glorious opportunities and victories.

What are some ideals which you *know*, but which you have not really striven to achieve? What are some goals which you know to be necessary and right, but which you have made little or no effort to reach? What are some Christian obligations, inescapably placed upon you by the teachings of Christ, which you have shirked with the soothing resolution to perform them one of these days? Because you are an intelligent Christian, you know without elaboration that procrastination is a deadly foe to maximum achievement and needs to be laid aside—*now*, not next week!

X

Until Peter laid aside *prejudice*, he was not as fully usable in God's plan for reaching lost people (Acts 10). The disciples would never have deigned to speak to the woman at the well of Sychar, because she was a woman of Samaria, toward whom all "good" Jews were prejudiced. Because the Jewish leaders were so bound by prejudice, they could not tolerate the unprejudiced teachings of Jesus. One of the factors which fashioned the cross on which Christ died was the sin of prejudice.

Prejudice *blinds*, so that the Christian cannot even see some obvious truths. Prejudice *deafens*, so that the Christian cannot even hear some calls of God to his heart. Prejudice *poisons* the Christian's thinking and emotions, so that amazing bitterness emanates from lip and life. Prejudice *paralyzes* the Christian's usefulness, so that God cannot use him in keeping with his abilities and in keeping with God's plan. Small wonder that the prejudiced Christian does not run the race victoriously!

Let us not confuse prejudice with conviction. Prejudice comes from two Latin words, *prae* (prior to) and *judicium* (the truth or judgment or justice). Therefore, prejudice may be defined as "an adverse opinion arrived at before the holder of that opinion has adequate knowledge on which to base his opinion, or an adverse opinion arrived at without just grounds for that opinion." It follows logically, therefore, that a prejudice can never be documented with fact or supported with justice.

Conviction, on the other hand, is a strong position or belief arrived at because of the truth available with which to sustain the position or belief. A conviction can be documented, sustained, and proved with indisputable fact always.

Prejudices toward individuals, toward types of preaching or types of music, toward wise organizational procedures in churches, and even toward progress of any sort have hampered so many local churches through the years. Many individual Christians have permitted their horizons to be narrowed, their hearts shrunk in compassion, and their spiritual usefulness circumscribed by prejudices. Like Peter, they will never be of maximum usefulness and inspiration to their day until their deterring prejudices are laid aside.

It would be well for all of us as Christians to run through our "Conviction Files" now to see how many items filed there would honestly have to be filed under the heading of "Prejudices." And, taking a look at the prejudices, we shall have to decide whether to keep them and lose the chance of maximum spiritual victory, or whether to lay them aside and increase the likelihood of wonderful spiritual advancement.

Are you satisfied with the quantity and the quality of the spiritual progress of your life? Do you feel that you are running the race victoriously? If the answer is "No," there must be something in your life which needs to be laid aside. If you did not find that something in the list of ten deterrents listed above, God *will* reveal to you what your trouble is, if you will ask him with the honest desire to know and with the honest intention to obey!

11. Can You Afford
That Emotion?

> *But I say unto you, Love your ene-*
> *mies, bless them that curse you, do*
> *good to them that hate you, and pray*
> *for them which despitefully use you*
> *and persecute you.*   Matthew 5:44

A GROUP OF US WERE EN ROUTE TO A
religious gathering in Stockholm, Sweden, in the summer of 1949. Though some of us had been to Europe
before, no one in our party had been there since the
conclusion of World War II in 1945. As we approached
London, the first stop on our itinerary, our hearts were
heavy with apprehension, for we feared that some of
the grand old buildings in which historic events had
occurred and around which so much of the sentiment
of English literature had clung would be missing, de-
stroyed by war.

Our apprehensions were justified; for, indeed,
some of those buildings were gone, and gaping holes
were there. Other buildings could be built in their

places, but those grand old landmarks of history and of literature were gone forever. We began to observe in the early days of our trip that the cost of war is so great, the loss so vast!

But, as grieved as we were for the high cost of war in London, we were amazed at the greater destruction which we found in western Germany: not just blocks or acres of destruction, but miles and miles of the most hopeless rubble imaginable. Though we had known that the British and American airmen had done a thorough job in fighting a desperate enemy, we had not realized during wartime that the destruction would be so vast. Though we were representatives of the winning side, and though we knew that our airmen had no alternative to raining destruction upon an enemy which threatened the peace of the world, we were still saddened deeply by the high cost of war, now so starkly revealed to our eyes.

As we sat at dinner one evening in a dining room reconstructed from the rubble, a member of our party observed, "Isn't war the highest-costing operation in which our world ever engages?" In studied reply, another member of our party rejoined, "But if there were no hate in men's hearts, there would be no war between nations." Immediately and unanimously we agreed that he was correct.

Though any nation will fight a defensive war without hating, no nation will put its heart into an aggressive war without having been taught to hate the intended victims of the aggression. Though the rulers themselves may be motivated by desires for expansion, for economic advantages, or for power, they know that the people will not put their hearts into an aggressive struggle unless they are taught to hate.

What did hate in the heart of our world cost during the years of World War II, and what is the continuing cost? The amount of money expended in preparation of armaments and in prosecution of the war effort was so large that it would be almost unpronounceable for the nonmathematician. The amount of money being spent each day now to care for the aftermath of that war is phenomenal. Just the monetary cost of that great holocaust of hate is proving to be so great that great-grand-children of today's youth will still be paying the bill!

In lives lost in the direct hostilities and from indirect results of the war, the estimates vary from twenty to fifty million. The ten million men lost in actual combat comprised the flower of the young manhood of the competing nations. This was a loss our world could not afford. Many contributions which these men would have made in all areas of life and progress will never be made, and our world will be much poorer as a result.

The emotional hurt of the war was tragic. Mothers bade only sons good-by, never to see them again on this earth. Wives kissed husbands good-by, and today have only lonely memories with which to try to fill the vacuum created as those men fell on battlefields. Children, who barely remember the dads who went away to war, have grown up bereft of a source of fellowship and strength for which there is no adequate substitute. One factor in the unprecedented wave of juvenile delinquency in the postwar years was the disruption of home security, regularity of family life, and normal affection.

The cultural loss to our world was so vast, too. The great universities of Europe were practically inoperative during those years, and many American men who normally would have had college experience either could not or did not have the opportunity of college training. Therefore, great books which might have been written will never be written; great drama which could have been produced will never be produced; great music which might have been composed will never be heard; great doctors, ministers, teachers, and other significant contributors to national and international welfare who would have come from normally functioning educational institutions will never be numbered among us. The loss to our world because of hate is vast, indeed!

If hate in the heart of an individual called "The World" brought so much hurt and cost, it follows that hate in any individual's heart will bring tragic cost to him. Though the cost of hate in the human heart is almost beyond calculation, there are at least three hurts which will come into the life of an individual who permits hate to live in his heart.

I

In the first place, hate in the heart will damage an individual's *physical* health. A wonderful specialist in internal medicine told me of some patients who were sure of ulcers and fearful of cancers in their stomachs, but whose diagnoses revealed neither ailment, and whose responses to medication and diet showed no improvement in the symptoms. Upon skilful penetration into the factors playing upon their lives, he found that, almost without exception, their hearts were filled with unwholesome attitudes toward other people. In the cases of the patients with hate-filled hearts, he gave this very frank advice: "Only the Great Physician, who taught us to love and forgive our enemies, can help you to be well again."

There are many authenticated records of people whose blood pressure became chronically high, or who developed dangerous heart action, or whose normal bodily functions were impaired because of hate in the heart. One allergist, greatly interested in the psychosomatic aspect of medicine, reported many instances of people with allergic symptoms whose real trouble was based in resentments, unforgiving attitudes, or outright hate. Hate in the heart *will* hurt one's physical health!

II

Hate in the human heart will impair one's *mental* health. Psychiatrists are constantly aware of the possibility of hate complexes in the background of behavior problems which they seek to diagnose. Many of them have gathered extensive evidence for the contention that hate in the heart affects mental health, sometimes .

even to the point of requiring institutional treatment.

One counselor described the effect of hate in the heart upon one's mental clarity with this very interesting analogy:

> Hate is like a fire in the heart. The fire sends smoke up to the brain, clouding the brain's capacity to think clearly in any instance related directly or indirectly to the object of hate. Therefore, thinking in that area is distorted and perverted; yet, the individual is so sure that his perverted impression is correct that he tells it for truth; thus, mere fiction has become as real as life to him. He has lost mental capacity for fair, objective, safe thinking.

Still another counselor offered the observation that if in hospitals for mental treatment there were missing all of those who came there because of too-long-entertained emotions of resentment and hate, those hospitals would lose a tremendous number of patients and would no longer be overcrowded. The prisons have a heavy population of people who hated so hotly that impulsively or deliberately they broke society's laws. Law violators often plead in the courts, "I just blacked out . . . I was temporarily insane. . . ." How high is the cost of hate to mental health!

III

The third high cost of hate in the human heart is the *spiritual* hurt which comes to the individual. To focus our thinking immediately upon the reason for the spiritual hurt of hate in the heart, let us face this indisputable fact: *it is a sin in the sight of God for the Christian to hate any other person in the world.* Astounding? Unreasonable? Impossible? Let us take a look at Christ's dealing with hate.

In terms which are so clear that they can be neither mistaken nor explained away, Christ taught that the Christian's obligation to love people goes far beyond his loving loved ones and lovable ones. The Christian is bidden to love even his enemies! More than that, the Christian is bidden to pray for those enemies and to return good for evil in dealing with his enemies (Matt. 5:43–48). Those teachings of Jesus are unamended and unrevoked: they are personally binding upon every Christian. The kind of Christian love which Jesus taught and practiced automatically precludes hate in the heart.

Then, too, Christ practiced so gloriously the principle of loving and forgiving enemies. While hanging on the cross in excruciating pain, after having been abused in the vilest way through hours of trial and humiliation, he lifted his heart to heaven with this prayer for his enemies: "Father, forgive them; for they know not what they do" (Luke 23:34). After having been misunderstood, maligned, misquoted, misinterpreted, spat upon, smitten in anger, mocked with a crown of thorns and a purple robe, flogged, sent out the way of grief with his own cross, nailed in anger upon that cross, and then reviled with indignities and obscenities, he *still* did not hate!

In addition to his teaching to instruct us and his example to inspire us, we have the promise of unlimited power to assist us in obeying his teachings concerning love and forgiveness. "Lo, I am with you alway" (Matt. 28:20). "For with God all things are possible" (Mark 10:27). "I can do all things through Christ which strengtheneth me" (Phil. 4:13).

Therefore, regardless of how great the wrong may be which has been done to you, how unjust the treatment which you have received, how humiliating the experience has been out of which hate came into your heart, you do not have the right to hate people if you are a Christian. To say that you are not obliged to relinquish hate is to say that you are not obliged to take the teaching and example of Jesus seriously. To say that you cannot do it is to charge that the power available to you from God is inadequate, and that charge approaches blasphemy! You *ought* to resolve to relinquish hate; you *can* do it with God's help. The only question now is, *will* you be big enough, Christlike enough to do it? If your answer is yes, you will have achieved one of life's great victories; you will have brought inspiration to others with similar problems; your life will have become a great credit to Christianity.

IV

There is always a peculiarly refreshing and challenging quality in the experiences of people who are our contemporaries, facing the problems which we face, who achieve victories possible for all of us. Some reader with a problem of hate may be encouraged to know of some contemporary twentieth-century Christians who have proved that this first-century teaching of Christ is attainable in our day.

A Christian who had given his life to an institution for many years in devoted, dedicated service received from the head of that institution an unquestionably wrong treatment. It amounted to demotion and humiliation, though the man had given many years of outstanding service, going always beyond the call of duty. He was unquestionably wronged, but as a Christian he did not have the right to hate.

For several years, however, he plunged into the wilderness of keen personal hate toward his superior officer. He became preoccupied and obsessed with the wrong which he had received. He almost lost his way in the wilderness: for years he hardly read his Bible, he did no real praying, he had no desire to help anyone else spiritually. Eventually he lost peace of mind and joy of heart. Hate had cost him everything which had earlier made life happy.

In a fine experience of consideration, confession, and rededication he came to follow his Lord's teaching and example in forgiveness. Warmth of heart returned, tenderness of concern came back, and a new light came into his face and eyes. He had the feeling of having been released from the power of a demon. How vast had been the dreadful cost of hate in that Christian's life!

Guideposts for March, 1959, carried as its feature article one of the most stirring episodes of Christian forgiveness ever to occur in the heart of a follower of Jesus. You will be glad always that you read the story in its entirety; so, avail yourself of a copy of that excellent little publication and read the story in detail.[1] The story is of Karl and Edith Taylor, for many years happily married and deeply devoted.

A government transfer necessitated Karl's going to Okinawa for an indeterminate period. While there, he became associated with a native Japanese girl to whom, evidently, he became obligated. He obtained by proxy a Mexican divorce from Edith, whose devotion to him on the home front had continued to be a thing of beauty. One can imagine Edith's consternation upon receiving, without any prior intimation, a letter from Karl with the news of his divorce and remarriage.

Though the average Christian would have screamed vengeance and would have gone to great lengths to obtain it, Edith sat where she was until she had thought the entire matter through and had resolved not only not to hate Karl but to forgive him, and to continue to love him, despite her broken heart.

In her reply to Karl, she suggested that they continue writing as heretofore, sharing with each other the day-by-day details which they had always shared. Easy and comfortable letters passed to and fro. In 1951 a little daughter was born to Karl and Aito, his Japanese wife. In 1953 a second little daughter came. Gifts flowed generously from Edith, and letters and pictures of the little daughters came from Karl and Aito, who had become so fond of Edith through the correspondence that she had begun to call her "Aunt Edith."

Then came the sad news of Karl's impending death from a malignancy. Karl's letters bore a sense of concern that his little daughters not be obliged to grow up on Okinawa. He had been saving money to educate them in America, but the hospital bills were eating up his savings. Edith knew that there was one more thing which she could do to ease the anxiety of his fleeting hours: she could volunteer to accept Karl's little daughters for rearing in America.

In a magnificent translation of the spirit of Jesus, Edith wrote to suggest to Karl that if Aito were willing to part with the little girls, she would be willing to take them and to rear and educate them. Some months following Karl's death, Aito voluntarily sent the little girls to Edith.

After a time, Edith discovered that she could not work and be an adequate mother to the little girls; therefore, in a triumph of Christian grace rarely ever seen since Golgotha's forgiveness, she obtained the help of a distinguished writer and subsequent help through her congressman for a congressional enabling act to permit the Japanese mother to come to live with her and the little daughters. They live together today in a northeastern city—an irresistible example of Christian love and forgiveness.

There have been so many other inspiring instances of triumph over hate in our time. There was a devoted husband whose beautiful wife was brutally assaulted and ravished by a man of another race. He went through a virtual hell of hate to the point of wanting to commit murder. In a suggested restudy of the behavior of Christ toward vile and malicious wrongdoers, this man came through to forgiveness and peace.

There was a magnificent woman, left widowed and with little children, who was cheated of her husband's part of the family fortune. Though she was turned out to make her way unaided, she maintained a completely forgiving spirit and has sought, through these years, with Christian compassion to win her malefactors to Christ.

There were many American servicemen who were submitted to great cruelties in Japanese prison camps; yet they kept remembering that their adversaries would not treat them thus if they knew Christ. Some of these American prisoners so loved and forgave that, upon their release from imprisonment, they resolved to give financial aid to Christian missions in Japan. Several of those men have since returned to Japan as Christian missionaries.

This galaxy of heroes and heroines of Christian love and forgiveness had access to no more power than that available to you and me. What they did in following the example and teaching of Jesus, we can do. Since the teaching, example, and power of Christ challenge us to forgiveness, we ought to forgive; for no Christian can afford the high cost of hate in his heart!

12. Are You Afraid to Die?

> *The last enemy that shall be destroyed is death. . . .*
> *Then shall be brought to pass the saying that is written, Death is swallowed up in victory.*
>
> 1 CORINTHIANS 15:26,54

AN EARNEST CHRISTIAN WOMAN APproached me and, with some reluctance, disclosed a fear which I have found to be rather surprisingly widespread among Christians. Said she, "Though I know that I am a Christian and that I ought not to be afraid of death, for some strange reason, I *am* afraid to die." She felt that somewhere along the way she had missed the concept of death which would make such fears illogical and unlikely. She was but one of many Christians who entertain this fear of death.

Are you afraid to die? At the very outset, let us point out that it is not normal for a person in good strength and usefulness to *want* to die. What is, doubtless, life's strongest urge, the urge to self-preservation, would be missing if one in excellent health and potential for successful living should actually want to die. Therefore, no one needs to be reluctant to admit that he is not eager to die. It is illogical, however, for one who belongs to the Christ who conquered death and the grave to be afraid to die.

Therefore, if one is afraid to die, one of three circumstances must be responsible for the fear: (1) he is *unsaved* and, therefore, not prepared to meet God; (2) he is *unconsecrated,* following Christ afar off in personal living and, therefore, ashamed to face God; (3) he is *uninformed* concerning the true nature of death for the Christian and, therefore, erroneously afraid of death.

I

The individual who has not trusted Christ and is, therefore, unsaved ought to be afraid to die, for he knows from the unmistakable clarity of the teachings of God's Word that standing in the presence of God without salvation will bring a dreadful sentence. Some teachings of the Bible in that regard are these:

> But he answered and said, Verily I say unto you, I know you not (Matt. 25:12).

> Depart from me, ye cursed, into everlasting fire, prepared for the devil and his angels. . . . And these shall go away into everlasting punishment (Matt. 25:41,46).

I tell you, Nay: but, except ye repent, ye
shall all likewise perish (Luke 13:3).

Those who have stood at the bedsides of unsaved
people who were conscious that life was slipping away
have shared with others the impression of tragedy seen
in the faces and heard in the voices of the dying ones.
There was evident the realization that the time to face
God had come, and that they had rejected—often, perhaps—the only hope of standing in God's presence
justified and unafraid. It is entirely understandable
that an unsaved person should be afraid to die: he
ought to be afraid!

II

If, however, the person entertaining the fear of
death is a Christian, he ought not to be afraid to die, for
he does not need to be afraid. Yet, if that Christian has
been living a life of disobedience, consciously and con-
tinuously following Christ afar off in his daily living, it
is not surprising that he should be ashamed at the
thought of coming face to face with the Christ whom he
has so regularly offended. It is the same sense of shame
with which a child is familiar in being brought face to
face with parents whose rules or wishes he has repeat-
edly disobeyed.

A brilliant young professional man had been found
to be in tragic violation of some laws. His case would
soon come to the attention of the public. A sordid trial
and possible penal sentence confronted him. He came

to confide his tragedy to his pastor. The pastor suggested immediately that the young man's father be called, so that the shock of public disclosure would not find him unprepared.

With an agony of remorse and with a flood of tears the young man cried out: "Oh, I would rather die than to face my father. He taught me so wisely and well, and I have no excuse for the shame which I have brought upon myself and him!" The prospect of coming face to face with one whose teaching, devotion, and example he had flagrantly dishonored brought an almost unbearable sense of shame. A similar feeling of overwhelming shame should touch the Christian of disobedient life when he thinks of coming face to face with Jesus at the hour of death. His fear of death grows out of the disobedience of his life.

On the other hand, the obedient Christian, though fully aware of his infinite unworthiness of Christ's gift of grace, can have a sense of thrill in prospect of coming face to face with the Saviour, Teacher, Pattern, and Lord of his life. The joy of an excited wife at the airport, waiting to welcome her husband home after a long mission overseas, is a comparison. Because she has been full of love and faithful devotion to him, she is not only not afraid to see him, she is almost delirious with joy at the thought of seeing him. The finer the Christian's fellowship with Jesus and the fuller his obedience, the less will be his fear of meeting Jesus and the greater his joy.

It is, therefore, understandable that the unconsecrated Christian is afraid to die: his shame makes him afraid.

III

If the Christian who is warmly close to Jesus in his daily living is afraid to die, the reason for the fear must be that he is uninformed concerning the true nature of death for the Christian. Let us point out, first, some things which death is *not*.

Death is not the "end of it all"; it is, rather, the beginning of the main part of the eternal life which became the Christian's possession when he opened his heart to the Saviour. Death is not a demotion into the earth; it is, instead, a promotion process through which the Christian moves unfettered into the presence of God. Death is not a dead-end street in the Christian's journey; it is, instead, a doorway from earth to heaven. Death is not a defeat for the Christian; it is, instead, a glorious victory, made possible to the Christian through Christ's victory over death and the grave. It is not, therefore, a tragedy: it is a triumph. It is not something awful: it is something glorious, for which the Christian will thank God through all the years of heaven.

If the Christian will remember that death is merely a necessary vestibule through which he passes into the incomparable joy of heaven, he will begin to concentrate upon the magnificent privilege of being in heaven, rather than upon the momentary discomfort which physical death may bring.

The meaning of heaven is so vast and so wonderful that it is impossible for us to conceive of its magnificence while on this earth. At best, we can only summarize some of the attractive realities which heaven will bring. Perhaps a listing of a few of the things which heaven will make possible will help the uninformed Christian to drop his fear of death.

First, heaven will make possible a time of reunion with the wonderful Christians whom we have known and loved on the earth, and who have preceded us in death. I remember with inspiring freshness a conversation with a magnificent Christian whose doctors had told her that she could not be cured. Her radiant joy in the thought of seeing her wonderful husband soon and of fellowship with a host of other Christian friends who had preceded her to heaven simply overflowed and touched those in her hospital room with a thrill we had rarely felt before.

Though this writer does not presume to offer explanations of what forms we shall have in heaven, he does believe from the teachings of the New Testament that we shall know people in heaven whom we have known here. That being true, the prospect of joyous reunion with long-missed loved ones adds a dimension of happiness to the meaning of heaven which begins to minimize the fear of the physical death which admits us!

Second, heaven will be a time of discovery; for we shall have the thrill of meeting great Christians of the centuries whom we never had the opportunity to know personally, and to discover so many wonderful, though humble ones, of whom we had never even heard. Think of seeing Peter, John, Paul, Timothy, and the great host of early, heroic Christians. Think of seeing the martyrs who, through the centuries, so gloriously laid down their lives in the name of Jesus. Think of the inexpressible thrill of seeing Jesus! This glorious time of discovery will probably evoke from our hearts many times the expression, "Oh, why was I ever afraid or reluctant to die?"

Third, heaven will be a time of fulfilment. There will be nothing missing from the experience that the heart could desire, and more things than the imaginative minds of our greatest dreamers ever thought of will come to us in eternal succession. With the omnipotence of God around us, with the omniscience of God available, we shall never be limited in ability to achieve or to understand. Joy will be complete; peace will be perfect; achievement will be maximum; nothing will be lacking. Small wonder that the heavenly hosts are pictured as bursting into glorious song: the joy of fulfilment must overwhelm heaven's hosts constantly.

A wonderful Christian who had walked with Jesus through sixty years now lay near death. Her devoted daughters were right and left of her bed, watching anxiously and listening carefully for any syllable of conversation. They were aware that she could hardly live longer than a few hours more.

Suddenly the lovely one lifted both hands upright, and the daughters grasped them in fondness, sensing an attempt at farewell. Then a marvelous smile came to the dying one's face and she said, with a clarity of speech which she had not had for days, "Oh, I never dreamed it would be so wonderful!" With that, her hands fell limp; her pulse was no more, for she had walked into the presence of Jesus.

When I later offered condolence to one of the daughters, she said, with a new and wonderful peace glowing in her face, "I shall never again be afraid to die; for I was looking into Mother's face when she came to death, and I saw a commixture of surprise, joy, and victory which led me to know that she had found that death was merely a bridge to glory."

Two beautiful thoughts in poetry may well be tucked away into the hearts of all Christians of us as we march inexorably toward death, hand in hand with Jesus:

> And so for me there is no sting of death,
>   And so the grave has lost its victory.
> It is but crossing with abated breath
>   And white, set face—a little strip of sea,
> To find the loved ones waiting on the shore
> More beautiful, more precious than before.[1]
>   ELLA WHEELER WILCOX

> There is no Death! What seems so is transition;
>   This life of mortal breath
> Is but a suburb of the life elysian,
>   Whose portal we call Death.[2]
>   HENRY WADSWORTH LONGFELLOW

Notes

Poem Facing Preface

1. From *The Greatest of These* by Jane Merchant. Copyright 1951, 1954 by Pierce & Washabaugh. By permission of Abingdon Press.

Chapter Four

1. From a sermon titled "Will Religion Destroy Us?" Used by permission of Dr. Cowling. Copies of sermon available from Second Baptist Church, Little Rock, Arkansas.

2. John Baillie, *A Diary of Private Prayer* (New York: Charles Scribner's Sons, 1949).

3. David Head, *He Sent Leanness* (New York: Macmillan Co.).

Chapter Eleven

1. Used by permission of *Guideposts,* 3 West 29th Street, New York 1, New York.

Chapter Twelve

1. Ella Wheeler Wilcox, "And So for Me," from *Collected Poems of Ella Wheeler Wilcox.* (Chicago: W. B. Conkey Co., 1920).

2. Henry Wadsworth Longfellow, from "Resignation," *Complete Poetical Works* (Boston: Houghton Mifflin Co., 1893).